Breath Lines

JAN SCHREIBER

Breath
Lines

HOW
POEMS
WORK
AND
WHY
THEY
MATTER

Louisiana State University Press
Baton Rouge

Published by Louisiana State University Press
lsupress.org

Designer: Barbara Neely Bourgoyne
Typeface: Whitman

Cover illustration courtesy AdobeStock/DK_2020.

Library of Congress Cataloging-in-Publication Data
Names: Schreiber, Jan, 1941– author.
Title: Breath lines : how poems work and why they matter / Jan Schreiber.
Description: Baton Rouge : Louisiana State University Press, 2025. |
    Includes bibliographical references and index.
Identifiers: LCCN 2024048211 (print) | LCCN 2024048212 (ebook) | ISBN
    978-0-8071-8393-9 (cloth) | ISBN 978-0-8071-8402-8 (paperback) | ISBN
    978-0-8071-8431-8 (epub) | ISBN 978-0-8071-8432-5 (pdf)
Subjects: LCSH: Poetry. | Poetics. | LCGFT: Essays. | Literary criticism.
Classification: LCC PN1031 .S385 2025 (print) | LCC PN1031 (ebook) | DDC
    808.1—dc23/eng/20241230
LC record available at https://lccn.loc.gov/2024048211
LC ebook record available at https://lccn.loc.gov/2024048212

for Frances

Poets survive in fame.
But how can substance trade
The body for a name
Wherewith no soul's arrayed?

No form inspires the clay
Now breathless of what was
Save the imputed sway
Of some Pythagoras,

Some man so deftly mad
His metamorphosed shade,
Leaving the flesh it had,
Breathes on the words they made.

—J. V. CUNNINGHAM

Contents

Preface

This book is not a systematic treatise expounding a theory of poetry. Nor is it an invective against presumed errors of taste or judgment that might be found in the writings of others. It had its origin in a series of talks I presented at an annual symposium called The Critical Path. Originally centered at Western Colorado University, the symposium brings together poets of a critical bent who exchange ideas on whatever topics each speaker finds enticing. The chapters in this book are thus a series of forays into the dense forest of poetry. Each is intended to illuminate something important in a way that might guide other readers toward insight and appreciation.

Despite their unsystematic origins, these essays are not merely random sallies. Several are concerned with voices in poetry: what fictional persons speak, whether the poet, in the first person, appears in the poem, and whether it is possible to write an interesting and meaningful poem in which no one at all shows up. Other essays focus on the sounds of poems—for the distinguishing feature of most poems, in contrast to prose, is that the sound of the spoken words plays an essential role in their effect. Readers must *hear* a poem to grasp it. Still other essays recognize what many readers of poetry find most troubling: some poems are devilishly hard to understand. Hard but not impossible. These essays offer a guide for the perplexed. I recommend them. There are rewards at the end.

Finally, because we've experienced a century of tumult in the arts, with rebels urging their peers to sweep away old approaches to music, poetry, and the graphic arts, and to "make it new," some of these essays attempt to take stock and assess what has been gained and lost in the revolution and what the future might hold. Over many decades, some writers doggedly produced work in traditional styles, while others resolutely jettisoned those styles and forged new ones. What are we left with, and where do we go from here?

Some readers of this book are likely to write the next chapters.

INTRODUCTION

1

SOURCES OF DELIGHT
What We Respond to When We Respond to Poetry

When I was seventeen years old and barely aware of poetry, with no idea what good poetry might be, or even what if anything might please me, a friend, just back from his English class, rushed breathlessly into my room at boarding school, book in hand, and cried, "Listen to this!"

> I caught this morning morning's minion, king-
>   dom of daylight's dauphin, dapple-dawn-drawn Falcon, in his riding
>   Of the rolling level underneath him steady air, and striding
> High there, how he rung upon the rein of a wimpling wing . . .[1]

and I felt a chill go up my spine. Poetry could do that? Sometimes it takes a spectacular gesture to get one's attention. In the more than sixty years since, I've come to appreciate—and strive in my own work for—far subtler effects, but I remain convinced that poetry, while sometimes narrative, sometimes meditation, sometimes rational argument, sometimes dream, is at bottom a practice of rhetoric. In this book I want to look at rhetorical technique and the ways it fuses with the denotative and connotative meanings of poems to arrest our attention and stay in our minds, or—to put it less artfully—to move us and to thrill us.

The book is not intended as a systematic guide to rhetorical tropes—something as tedious as it is unoriginal. It's intended rather as a provocation to readers looking to develop or refine a nose for the remarkable passage, as an oenophile might develop a nose for superior wines. But because I want to start from consensus and work toward discovery, my first illustrations come not from out-of-the-way rarities but from works nearer at hand, though not on the tip of most tongues, from the century just past.

In calling attention to them I hope to illustrate my conception of a critic's central obligations. These stem from the defining characteristics of a poem, of a construction in words that, as David Rothman puts it,[2] both says something and does something. To make that formula a little more explicit, we can say that a poem, being a creature of language, has meanings that are conveyed through linguistic means, and being also a creature of sound (which is not incidental as in prose but structural), has the potential to affect the hearer's sensibility through auditory stimulus, including rhythmic patterning, the repetition or modulation of speech sounds, and the strategic deployment of silence. To the extent that a poem exploits that potential, it is up to the critic to analyze—or at any rate to understand—what is being said (unless of course he cannot understand it, in which case, if he is honest, he will say so), and also to observe how the sounds of the poem do or do not contribute to its total impact. Sound, which we often hear only in our minds as we read, has a manifold effect that is hard to put into words. On a simple level it can be calming and slightly hypnotic; at times it can heighten tension; occasionally it can illustrate or imitate a meaning; and very often it serves to organize what we are hearing—which during the course of the poem is, if we are attentive, the world of our experience.

This division between sound and meaning is not the same as that between rhetoric and plain speech. Rhetoric comprises various ways of organizing and presenting meaning as well as the manipulation of strictly sonic elements. It is a more inclusive term with a long history in critical discussions. But rhythm alone—patterns of sound—can powerfully affect a reader's sensory response. In what follows I will frequently speak of rhetoric and rhetorical techniques, but we should remember that these stem from the poet's ability to manipulate both sound and sense and that, at least in most of the poems we'll be looking at, the purely sonic patterning—one aspect of rhetoric—greatly exceeds what is ordinarily encountered in prose.

To get down to cases, consider Wallace Stevens's "The Idea of Order at Key West," one of the landmarks of twentieth-century poetry.[3] For all its seductive language, the poem is structured like a legal brief, with clear syntactic markers showing just where we are in the progress of the argument. The question before the court is whether a particular occurrence—a song beside the sea—is natural or contrived. Stevens wants to draw a clear distinction between the two options, and to persuade us that what we have been hearing—a woman singing—goes far beyond mere natural phenomena, however much it might incorporate their influences. Thus the first line of the poem states the entire case of the brief in a succinct sentence of ten syllables:

She sang beyond the genius of the sea.

And we are to understand "genius" as encompassing the ideas of "spirit," "nature," and "utmost capability." A series of declarative sentences follow, each advancing a component of the claim. The advocate asserts that the sea, with its natural sounds, did not take on the features of mind or voice. The assertion is coupled with an arresting simile: "Like a body wholly body, fluttering / Its empty sleeves." The essential human element, the animating spirit, is absent.

The poem asserts next that neither the sea nor the singer was a disguise (mask) for the other, that the sounds of singing and of water did not blend but were distinct, and that even if wind and water sounds echoed in the singer's phrases, "it was she and not the sea we heard." I am deliberately reducing the poem to its bare rational statements, but this is not hard to do, for the syntax is plain and the sentences are straightforwardly declarative.

Having made its point that the song contained an element quite different from the sea-sound, the poem addresses the obvious question: "Whose spirit is this?" and proceeds to consider the options that the spirit was only the "dark voice of the sea" or "the outer voice of sky / And cloud." In that case it would have been repetitious and without meaning ("sound alone"). But in fact it had an additional and remarkable quality—and this is the part of the argument that readers most often miss. It had the force to make us see things differently. It enhanced vision and "made / The sky acutest at its vanishing." In effect, it created a world that had not existed before.

At this point the poem calls in an expert witness, Ramon Fernandez, though he doesn't get a chance to speak. But in addressing him the advocate rounds out his argument: see how the lights in the fishing boats lying at anchor have "portioned out the sea," creating order where there was only randomness and in the process shaping our experience of the night. And, it is implied, just as a simple man-made thing like a boat light (or, we might recall, a jar in Tennessee) can transform its surroundings, so can a song. In that way the human spirit achieves finer distinctions ("ghostlier demarcations") and sharper perceptions ("keener sounds").

So much for the argument; what do the rhetoric and the sound patterns add? The poem is in iambic pentameter. It starts out seemingly in blank verse, without rhymes at the line-ends. But very soon rhyme appears—at first hardly noticed, as when "ocean" at the end of the first section chimes with "motion" four lines earlier; then unmistakably in the second section, when "heard" is echoed four times in five lines.

> The sea was not a mask. No more was she.
> The song and water were not medleyed sound
> Even if what she sang was what she heard,
> Since what she sang was uttered word by word.
> It may be that in all her phrases stirred
> The grinding water and the gasping wind;
> But it was she and not the sea we heard.
>
> For she was the maker of the song she sang.
> The ever-hooded, tragic-gestured sea
> Was merely a place by which she walked to sing.

Coupled with its irregular but persistent rhymes, the poem gives us complex alliteration, as when three initial m's are followed by five initial c's ("its mimic motion / Made constant cry, caused constantly a cry") or alternating g's and w's alliterate in "the grinding water and the gasping wind." This is not to suggest that these effects contribute to the poem's meaning, but that they are part of the hypnotic, incantatory quality in which the poem clothes its rational argument.

That quality is furthered by the use of what we've come to call Homeric epithets: twinned adjectives in which the second element is often a past participle, as in "The ever-hooded, tragic-gestured sea," and by the strategic repetition of words:

> If it was only the dark voice of the sea . . .
> . . . ↓   ↓
> If it was only the outer voice of sky
>   ↓
> And cloud, of the sunken coral water-walled,

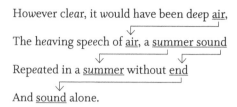

However clear, it would have been deep air,
The heaving speech of air, a summer sound
Repeated in a summer without end
And sound alone.

Here repeated words or phrases are joined by arrows; repeated sounds are noted with italics. (Note too that even the Homeric epithets can be inverted: the "tragic-gestured sea" is matched by the "sunken coral, water-walled.") Thus among a few blank-verse lines, lacking end-rhyme, there are densely interconnecting patterns of consonance and repetition.

An exhaustive analysis of the rhetoric of this poem would be exhausting. But I will note one more device: the progressive intensification of words presented as if they were synonyms, somewhat in the manner of Lincoln's "we cannot dedicate, we cannot consecrate, we cannot hallow this ground." Stevens's three words are also verbs, but in participle form: "Arranging, deepening, enchanting night." The first is an order of space; the second an order of emotion or perception; the third an order of the spirit. We accept the first, so we are led to accept the second, and then the third. Lincoln and Stevens were both lawyers. They knew how to insert the thin end of the wedge and take advantage of the opening.

■　■　■　■

Let us move from the orator frankly contriving to seduce with words and listen now to a portion of a modern narrative poem in which instruction and delight are fused. Derek Walcott has a singular ability to write about the world as if it were a poem, and at the same time to treat the mechanics of poetry as an aspect of life itself. In the course of narrating his wide-ranging epic *Omeros*, a Homeric tale of the adventures of West Indian fishermen, he encounters the spirit of his long-dead father, who walks with him through the harbor streets of St. Lucia, Walcott's birthplace. As they stroll, his father recalls the labors of local women who toted loads of coal to the ships that visited the ports of St. Lucia:

"The carriers were women, not the fair, gentler sex.
Instead, they were darker and stronger, and their gait
was made beautiful by balance, in their ascending

the narrow wooden ramp built steeply to the hull
of a liner tall as a cloud, the unending
line crossing like ants without touching for the whole

day. That was one section of the wharf, opposite
your grandmother's house where I watched the silhouettes
of these women, while every hundredweight basket

was ticked by two tally clerks in their white pith-helmets
and the endless repetition as they climbed the
infernal anthracite hills showed you hell, early."

His father turns then to draw an explicit parallel between the work of those
women and the task his son faces of writing poems that will last:

"Because Rhyme remains the parentheses of palms
shielding a candle's tongue, it is the language's
desire to enclose the loved world in its arms;

or heft a coal-basket; only by its stages
like those groaning women will you achieve that height
whose wooden planks in couplets lift your pages

higher than those hills of infernal anthracite.
There, like ants or angels, they see their native town,
unknown, raw, insignificant. They walk, you write;

keep to that narrow causeway without looking down,
climbing in their footsteps, that slow, ancestral beat
of those used to climbing roads; your own work owes them

because the couplet of those multiplying feet
made your first rhymes. Look, they climb, and no one knows them;
they take their copper pittances, and your duty

from the time you watched them from your grandmother's house
as a child wounded by their power and beauty
is the chance you now have, to give those feet a voice."

Both rhyme and meter, in this telling, come from the plodding feet of those women, and poems result not just from inspiration but also from relentless, conscientious labor. It is an *ars poetica* unusual in our day, when inspiration is still prized over careful craftsmanship, but in Walcott's voice it is both moving and a challenge to himself and his fellow writers.

．．．．

I want to turn now to two less famous poems that illustrate by their differences the strong role played by diction and sonic patterning.

Bruce Weigl's "Snowy Egret" might well be called a short story in thirty-four lines.[4] It's told in a language hard to distinguish from prose, and it shares with the short story form a concrete situation in which something happens that connects the past, the present, and a projected future. The action is straightforward: the narrator is wakened in the night to find a neighbor boy down near the shore, burying a snowy egret he has just shot, and overcome with sorrow and fear. Sorrow for having killed the bird, and fear for what his father might do if he finds out. The narrator comments on the scene and by interpreting what he describes assumes some of the functions of the traditional poet.

However, the poem is not in verse. It is a poem in that it fulfills the looser modern definition: *a short, intense piece of writing evoking strong emotion in brief compass.* In general it is unmetered. There are patches of what can be construed as iambic meter, but similar patches occur in many random passages of prose, even in the daily paper. It is hard to see a conscious metrical shaping at work, except in the third line:

and in the moon he's blasted a snow egret

(where the substitution of "moon" for "moonlight" and "snow" for "snowy" indicates a pull toward iambic pentameter) and again in the poem's final lines—

wiping out from the blue face of the pond
what he hadn't even known he loved, blasting
such beauty into nothing.

—where the penultimate line is scannable as iambic pentameter with an anapestic first foot and a trochaic substitution at the end. In fighting the usual pattern, "blasting" commands attention, and the last line, with only three iambic feet, feels suitably abrupt. (I note in passing, as have others, that many ostensibly free-verse poems drop into iambic meter in their closing lines, as if to take advantage of the extra force and ease of recall that meter imparts.)

The poem achieves its considerable pathos without attempting large generalizations. The lines just quoted are a kind of summation, and they are introduced by the poem's closest approach to an inclusive comment: "What a time we share, that can make a good boy steal away." Instead of arresting expressions the poem gives us physical details: the "dewy grass," the egret's "blood-spattered wings," the incongruous "man's muscled shoulders" on the distraught boy. As with most good fiction, the feeling of this poem stays with the reader, even if the words do not.

And yet this straightforward narrative is not without rhetorical flourishes. The narrator relates the boy's words when explaining how he killed the bird without meaning to. And at first they seem like words, and even repetitions, a boy would really use:

> He says he only meant to flush it from the shadows,
> but only meant to watch it fly
> but the shot spread too far . . .

But then the boy's report is embellished by the language of a more sophisticated adult: "ripping into the white wings spanned awkwardly for a moment / until it glided into brackish death." These are the narrator's imaginings—he was not there when it happened, and the boy would not have said this—yet we accept and even welcome the elaboration. We're in the presence of another kind of rhetorical stroke: not the seductions of sound but the suffusion of detail, something done to convince us that we ourselves might have witnessed the event.

It is instructive to consider this poem in relation to another on a similar subject—the death of a beautiful bird by human hands. Despite a superficial resemblance, "Angle of Geese," by N. Scott Momaday, is fundamentally a different kind of artifact.

To start with, Momaday's poem has not one subject but two. In fact it offers an unusually clear example of a poem's ability to juxtapose two quite different situations and feelings so that they react against and comment upon each other. The conjunction is, in the poem's words, "more than language means," but the emotional meaning becomes evident as the poem proceeds. The immediate situation is the death of a child, about which the survivors find it difficult to speak.

> How shall we adorn
> Recognition with our speech?—
>   Now the dead firstborn
> Will lag in the wake of words.
>
>   Custom intervenes;
> We are civil, something more:
>   More than language means,
> The mute presence mulls and marks.
>
>   Almost of a mind,
> We take measure of the loss;
>   I am slow to find
> The mere margin of repose.

The second situation is a hunt during which a goose is shot and killed. It is told in the past tense, as if recalled at the present moment of sorrow. The beauty of geese in flight and the pathos of the dying bird are felt simultaneously and are presented "in the wake of" the talk of the child's death and the attendant grief.

>   And one November
> It was longer in the watch,
>   As if forever,
> Of the huge ancestral goose.
>
>   So much symmetry!
> Like the pale angle of time
>   And eternity.
> The great shape labored and fell.
>
>   Quit of hope and hurt,
> It held a motionless gaze,
>   Wide of time, alert,
> On the dark distant flurry.

The final line suggests not just the goose's death throes but all human attempts to survive as life flickers and ends.

Formally the poem is unusual. In each stanza except the fourth, lines one and three rhyme and are in headless iambic trimeter, which means they are five syllables long. Lines two and four, by contrast, are seven syllables each, unrhymed and to my ear unmetered except for the syllable count. The effect is one of order and control in the odd-numbered lines, set against a more open-ended, indeterminate form. It is not the case that each type of line applies to one of the situations the poem describes; the alternating scansions are carried through the entire poem, regardless of content. But the oscillation or weaving between more "closed" and more "open" forms offers a subliminal commentary on the experiences the poem is attempting to come to grips with. Not everything that can be felt can be contained. Hyper-awareness is not always subject to rule.

If the diction of Weigl's poem is that of the modern short story, the diction of Momaday's poem is that of elevated discourse. From the first two lines, which are nothing like conversational idiom, it is plain that we are in a realm of formal convention that does not imitate ordinary language but grants the adroit user the ability to express complex ideas in condensed form.

The scene is shown clearly, but from a long distance. We do not know whether it is warm or cold, we do not feel the marshy grasses or smell the autumnal air. All the components of the poem—grievers, hunters, and bird—are condensed to their essence. The poem is sober and the tone is one of solemn meditation.

Yet in the ostensibly plain style there is subtle rhetoric. We have alliteration: "More than language *means* / the *mute* presence *mulls* and *marks*." And in the next stanza, almost, mind, measure, mere, margin. "The mere margin of repose" is a phrase that strikes the awareness before its import registers. It refers to the small space amid the surges of grief where one can momentarily rest. Similarly, the grandest phrase in the poem, the "pale angle of time / And eternity" inspires awe even before it is understood. It is the point of death, where time stops and timelessness begins. And the wedge of geese, which seems to represent this point in the abstract, suddenly demonstrates it concretely, as the great goose falls and dies. The alliteration continues through the last stanza, with *hope, hurt,* and *held,* and the *dark distant* flurry.

The tools of this poem, then, are its exalted style, its striking and large-minded expressions, its metrical complexity, its rhyme and liberal use of alliteration, and its fusion of two experiences, one present and one past, into a single perception that exceeds the sum of its parts. What it sacrifices are the conversational style and the narrative method so ably used in Weigl's poem to render an immediate human interaction. Each poem has its excellences; we need not choose one over the other—only recognize the technical resources out of which those excellences emerge.

. . . .

What a poem *says* is its meaning; what a poem *does* is to convince, through all the resources of sound, rhythm, tone, and imitation at the poet's command. It is the combination of meaning and rhetoric that delights and moves, and it is the critic's onus to bring these elements to readers' attention in understanding and assessing any particular poem.

Later chapters in this book will focus more closely on various aspects of poetic technique in an attempt to reveal elements that contribute to understanding at both rational and emotional levels. For a poem, like language itself, engages profound feelings, but it does so both through our visceral responses to its sounds and through our sometimes rapid and sometimes hard-won comprehension of its meanings.

NOTES

1. Gerard Manley Hopkins, "The Windhover."
2. David Rothman, "The Dark Pool," *Contemporary Poetry Review,* November 2010.
3. The poem can be found at: poetryfoundation.org/poems/43431/the-idea-of-order-at-key-west.
4. "Snowy Egret" can be found at: thebeckoning.com/poetry/weigl/weigl5.html.

I. THE CONTENT OF POETRY

2

SOME POETIC STRATEGIES

And so each venture
Is a new beginning, a raid on the inarticulate

   —T. S. Eliot, "East Coker"

I want to clear up some confusion about the way poems convey information over time. Because they necessarily parcel out words sequentially, poems must present a thematic thread or story line. It is not always a clear thread, and sometimes a poem offers more than one. From the obvious fact that poems often do not proceed in a straightforward manner, controlled either by chronological narration or by syllogistic logic, observers have developed various theories and analogies to explain what is actually going on. As early as 1942, in *Philosophy in a New Key*, Susanne Langer attempted to model the movement of poems on music, thereby freeing poetic structure from its obligation to the principles of discursive logic.

> Though the *material* of poetry is verbal, its import is not the literal assertion made in the words, but *the way the assertion is made,* and this involves the sound, the tempo, the aura of association of the words, the long or short sequences of ideas, the wealth or poverty of transient imagery that contains them, the sudden arrest of fantasy by pure fact, or of familiar fact by sudden fantasy, the suspense of literal meaning by a sustained ambiguity resolved in the long-awaited keyword, and the unifying, all-embracing artifice of rhythm.[1]

Largely accepting Langer's thesis, but choosing to concentrate on linguistic structure, Donald Davie in *Articulate Energy* tries to show how syntax in particular—quite apart from the actual meaning of the sentences involved—might control the movement and import of a poem:

> Hence we have to say that poetic syntax is like music when its function is to please us by the fidelity with which it follows a "form of thought" through the poet's mind, *but without defining that thought*. . . . Now in poetry it is not so easy as in music to articulate without asserting, to talk without saying what one is talking about. But, as is well known, this difficulty was circumvented by the use of the objective correlative. . . .[2]

At another point he says,

> But there is also the question of strategy, of where and how to create the new metaphor or recreate the old so that it may have the greatest effect. The right strategy is not to reveal the metaphor, the concretion, in every word used, even in prepositions like "upon" or "outside." This is the strategy of some persons writing today; and the result is only an incessant and intolerable fidget.[3]

What Davie is seeking here is an understanding of the way a poem may appear to be about something, or at least to contain details that call certain conceptions to mind, while actually conveying ideas and often strong feelings about something else entirely. This is indeed a curious phenomenon that calls out for exploration. But to understand poetry merely as music, or to see its movements as determined primarily by syntax, is to ignore precisely those unique features that make language in fact *qua* language most capable of operating simultaneously on multiple channels.

Perhaps this is a good place to insert a caveat that should already be obvious: I will adopt here the naïve assumption that a text has discernible (though often multiple and often nested) meanings on which independent readers can largely agree; that far from being fundamentally indeterminate, or a locus of unresolvable ambiguities, as some deconstructionists liked to maintain, most poems offer statements assignable, sometimes admittedly with no little ingenuity, to what most of us can agree is a simulacrum of the real world. I'll acknowledge further that such statements often have an ethical dimension which can exert strong pressure on the reader's emotional response. That is my justification for taking seriously the views of some long-dead critics whose entire world view has been called into question by what was until recently a strong and influential academic voice.

All writers, and poets in particular, confront two seemingly contradictory aspects of human psychology when attempting to convey meaning. Readers (and listeners) respond most rapidly and viscerally to words that convey striking sensory images or impressions. The desire to reach readers with such immediacy lay behind the imagist agenda in which sensory, preferably visual impressions are paramount and their wider implications, if any, are unstated. So H.D. (Hilda Doolittle) would write in "Sea Iris":

Weed, moss-weed,
root tangled in sand,
sea-iris, brittle flower,
one petal like a shell
is broken,
and you print a shadow
like a thin twig.

But vivid language speaks to only one human need. The second imperative is to be stirred, to be moved beyond merely sensuous response. The reader seeks a deeper intellectual and emotional understanding of something manifestly important. T. S. Eliot, in his introduction to Valéry's *The Art of Poetry*, refers to this quality as "seriousness": "the question of how [a poem] is related to the rest of life in such a way as to give the reader the shock of feeling that the poem has been to him, not merely an experience, but a serious experience."[4]

So as readers we want to be struck—as if by a direct encounter with the tangible world—and then we want to be moved, to feel that our perceptions of things that deeply matter to us have been altered or expanded. The contradiction between the desire for an immediate response to physical stimulus and the urge to be touched on a deeper level motivates most of the strategies that poets employ. Obviously not all poems can accomplish both of these objectives with equal success, and not every poet sets out to do so in every poem she writes. But the capabilities that make such achievements possible, even within the small compass of the lyric, derive from language, and not just its syntactic and prosodic features but most especially its semantic structures.

It is the peculiar genius of language that its component words may readily be given extended—or even quite different—meanings. This capacity is the basis for all metaphor. It allows a writer to invest a word or phrase with ad hoc meanings that go well beyond accepted denotation. And just as a word can be used metaphorically, so can an entire passage, so that sentences that seem to mean one thing may instead (or in addition) mean something else entirely.[5] Such a capability was recognized, of course, by Langer and by Ernst Cassirer, her major philosophical influence, but its implications were not fully worked out. In her discussion of human linguistic communication, Langer introduces the term *discursiveness*, and says, "by reason of it, only thoughts which can be arranged in this peculiar order can be spoken at all; any idea which does not lend itself to this 'projection' is ineffable, incommunicable by means of words."[6] But we shall shortly examine several strategies for doing exactly that: verbally communicating ideas not in themselves amenable to linear (i.e. discursive) presentation.

This ability to shift meanings, to instantaneously create them or multiply them, informs both our everyday speech and our poetry. If a friend says, "We all felt a chill when she walked into the room," we know it isn't because someone turned up the air conditioning. And when Wallace Stevens writes, "Every time the bucks went clattering / Over Oklahoma / A firecat bristled in the way," some readers, with a little ingenuity, will deduce that he is describing a railroad train. Others, with still more ingenuity, will draw highly inventive conclusions.[7] But beyond the potential for creative ambiguity, this quality of language has a profound potential to affect the *structure* of poems. It frees the poet from the need to convey material in a strictly linear or discursive fashion and instead makes it possible to present two or more levels of meaning, and sometimes two or more narratives, at once.

Indeed, what most excites the Romantic imagination (still at play in contemporary poets and critics) is a poem that brings together disparate associations and manages to connect them by an intuitive leap. Such a feat is thought to reveal the hidden workings of the unconscious and in so doing to widen awareness, deepen insight, and heighten aesthetic pleasure. It is true that some poets are more ingenious—even profligate—in their associations than others. It is also true that a poem invoking remote associations risks losing its readers. Certain theories of poetry tend to encourage tangential associations, while others are less hospitable.

As a starting point, consider the ordinary sort of poem that makes no attempt to superimpose one narrative upon another. Such a poem lays out the details of an argument or description step by step. This is the simplest structure, usually found in short portraits, like Edwin Arlington Robinson's "Reuben Bright," or reasoned discourse in verse, like Don Paterson's "The Error":

> As a bird is to the air
> and the whale is to the sea
> so man is to his dream.
>
> His world is just the glare
> of the world's utility
> returned by his eye-beam.
>
> Each self-reflecting mind
> is in this manner destined
> to forget its element,
>
> and this is why we find
> however deep we listen
> that the skies are silent.

The poem is full of comparisons—bird is to air as whale is to sea as man is to dream—but the comparisons are illustrative; they do not tell an alternative story or direct the movement of the poem, which remains simply a short disquisition on human perception and its limits.

Or one can say X (physical description) and allow the feelings (Y) associated with X to fill the emotional space of the poem. This was the mission of Imagism, a program to which H.D., Pound, and Williams all adhered for a time. H.D.'s "Oread" will serve as an example.

> Whirl up, sea—
> Whirl your pointed pines.
> Splash your great pines
> On our rocks.
> Hurl your green over us—
> Cover us with your pools of fir.

By personifying the sea (using the second-person pronoun) and enhancing her description by equating waves with trees, H.D. adds a quality of awe-struck reverence to the brief poem and evokes an image of observers actually *forested* by the sea. But the poem makes no attempt to tell a second story—to propose (for example) the inundation of the shore as a stand-in for the devastation of one's life by overwhelming events, though readers may of course make inferences.

But I am concerned here, additionally and primarily, with the effect of associative language on the structure of poems. Without hoping to list exhaustively the possible channels in which poetic themes may be developed by such means, I will catalog here some of the most commonly used, offering some illustrations as I proceed.

1. X is like Y

One can make an entire poem out of a simile, saying, "This is like that." Such a statement is not a metaphorical disguise. The poet may revel in the connection between two seemingly dissimilar elements and play with the terms of the likeness, as Robert Frost does in "The Silken Tent" and as Richard Wilbur does in "Mind":

> Mind in its purest play is like some bat
> That beats about in caverns all alone,
> Contriving by a kind of senseless wit
> Not to conclude against a wall of stone.
>
> It has no need to falter or explore;
> Darkly it knows what obstacles are there,
> And so may weave and flitter, dip and soar
> In perfect courses through the blackest air.
>
> And has this simile a like perfection?
> The mind is like a bat. Precisely. Save
> That in the very happiest intellection
> A graceful error may correct the cave.

What seems to tell a second story in this poem is not the simile itself, but the implied comparison: bat is to cave as mind is to world. The turn comes when we discover our mistake: the true analogy is: bat is to cave as mind is to an *idea* of the world—an idea that is corrigible.

But a simile, however ingenious, will only get us so far as a structural basis for a poem. A poet who sees a remarkable likeness between two phenomena will soon need a more robust way of illustrating the truths of one through the actions of the other. That need leads him to allegory.

2. X means Y

One can write so that the nominal subject is understood to mean something else. This is an ancient and time-honored mechanism, the basis for lengthy poems like "The Faerie Queene." In spite of the danger that the "real" message (Y) can so dominate the ostensible message (X) that the latter will seem stilted and contrived, some writers are still able to use allegory with considerable skill and wit, as Melvin Tolson does in "The Sea-Turtle & the Shark,"[8] where the sea turtle clearly represents Black populations that have been swallowed by white society (the shark) and must free themselves through their own persistence, cunning, and strength. The poem makes no claim to literal truth, but asserts a psychological reality.

3. X reminds me of Y

Stepping beyond allegory, a poet can abandon the notion of a pre-established one-to-one correspondence between two sets of actions (the narrated events and the intended ones), and can instead simply assert an association—usually between a physical phenomenon (X) and a metaphysical or psychological one (Y)—allowing the one to illustrate or illuminate the other. This is the method of Matthew Arnold in "Dover Beach." The success of such poems will depend in part on whether the reader views the connection as ingenious or contrived. The danger is that the poet may find himself forced into an awkward gesture as he works to show the essential resemblance of Y to X. So Arnold, attempting to move from surf sounds to a reflection on the loss of faith, resorts to the language of a motivational speaker: "we / Find also in the sound a thought, / Hearing it by this distant northern sea."

Richard Wilbur handles the problem with more suavity in "Blackberries for Amelia" when he describes blossoms on berry vines:

small, five-petalled blooms of chalky white,
As random-clustered and as loosely strewn
As the far stars, of which we are now told
That ever faster do they bolt away,
And that a night may come in which, some say,
We shall have only blackness to behold.

Here the associative leap is made by means of a comparison which, however unexpected, is nonetheless psychologically plausible.

4. X implies Y

A more allusive approach is taken by Robert Lowell's poem "Water," in which a few hints allow readers to discern the true subject in a scenic description, and in the process to understand the poem's thrust on a more visceral level.

It was a Maine lobster town—
each morning boatloads of hands
pushed off for granite
quarries on the islands,

and left dozens of bleak
white frame houses stuck
like oyster shells
on a hill of rock,

and below us, the sea lapped
the raw little match-stick
mazes of a weir,
where the fish for bait were trapped.

Remember? We sat on a slab of rock.
From this distance in time
it seems the color
of iris, rotting and turning purpler,

but it was only
the usual gray rock

turning the usual green
when drenched by the sea.

The sea drenched the rock
at our feet all day,
and kept tearing away
flake after flake.

One night you dreamed
you were a mermaid clinging to a wharf-pile,
and trying to pull
off the barnacles with your hands.

We wished our two souls
might return like gulls
to the rock. In the end,
the water was too cold for us.

The first three stanzas are straight description; only the word "us" in the third
stanza suggests that someone other than the speaker is involved. The second
person is addressed in the fourth stanza, and the way the recollection is evoked
suggests a relationship that existed some time ago. However, these are only
hints; the focus remains on the physical scene of the shore and the rocks.

In the last three stanzas the human figures become slightly more prominent. The reference to the mermaid dream in the seventh stanza informs us
that the person addressed is female, and the mention of "two souls" in the
last stanza suggests a close bond. With only these clues, we recast the scene
in metaphoric terms: the sea becomes a force that envelops and wears away
even the solidest things; the woman imagines herself clinging to some stable
bulwark while trying to rid herself (or it) of afflictions. The rock—stability,
solidity—is the goal, but the water (experience, the world at large) proves in-
imical, and the relationship fails. All this is seen as a past event, not narrated
sequentially and in fact not really narrated at all. The poem creates an aura
of recollection and its associated feelings while keeping the ostensible gaze
focused resolutely on ocean, rocks, and gulls.

5. X and Y comment on each other

One can say both X and Y and have the larger meaning arise from their juxtaposition. A fine example occurs in Seamus Heaney's sestina "Two Lorries," in which a recollection of a lorry operated by a coalman who flirts with the poet's mother merges with the memory, much later during the "Troubles," of a second lorry that exploded in the town of Magherafelt, destroying the bus station. The perceptions of innocence, romance, and random violence are now fused for the reader and cannot be decoupled.

As a second example, consider Elizabeth Bishop's short poem "The Shampoo":

> The still explosions on the rocks,
> the lichens, grow
> by spreading, gray, concentric shocks.
> They have arranged
> to meet the rings around the moon, although
> within our memories they have not changed.
>
> And since the heavens will attend
> as long on us,
> you've been, dear friend,
> precipitate and pragmatical;
> and look what happens. For Time is
> nothing if not amenable.
>
> The shooting stars in your black hair
> in bright formation
> are flocking where,
> so straight, so soon?
> —Come, let me wash it in this big tin basin,
> battered and shiny like the moon.

One thread in this poem is the patterns of lichen formations on rocks. Another is the flecks of gray ("shooting stars") forming in the friend's hair. Both threads are tied to the inexorable progress of time, reflected in celestial motions. The final two lines of the poem bring the themes together with the intimate gesture of the proffered shampoo in the moonlike basin.

6. X is revealed to be Y

One can write ostensibly about a scene but it gradually becomes clear one is really writing about a more important matter. William Carlos Williams's well-known poem "The Yachts" provides a fine illustration. The first eight stanzas appear to concern themselves strictly with the preparations for a race among well-tended boats, although very subtle hints (sharp prows, ant-like crews) may seem like warnings in retrospect. But in the final three stanzas the scene becomes one of horror as the waves turn to a shambles of desperate, grasping arms and hands, of faces and bodies sliced through by the indifferent yachts.

The same strategy is employed on a smaller scale in Thom Gunn's "The Bed":

> The pulsing stops where time has been,
>   The garden is snow-bound,
> The branches weighed down and the paths filled in,
>   Drifts quilt the ground.
>
> We lie soft-caught, still now it's done,
>   Loose-twined across the bed
> Like wrestling statues; but it still goes on
>   Inside my head.

The first stanza helps to fix in the reader's mind the belief that the title refers to a flower-bed, seen in the depth of winter. But the second stanza makes it clear that the first must be understood metaphorically: the real scene is an actual bed, immediately following a sexual act.

7. Surreal X suggests real Y

One can describe an event or a scene that is superficially implausible or incomprehensible, and let the reader's ingenuity infer a rational situation or statement behind it. This is a popular contemporary style of which there are many variants. It places the onus on the reader to make sense of something that initially seems incoherent. An example is the poem "Glut" by Gerald Stern:

> The whole point was getting rid of glut
> for which I starved myself and lived with the heat down

and only shaved oh every five days and used
a blunt razor for months so that my cheek
was not only red but the hair was bent not cut
for which I then would be ready for the bicycle
and the broken wrist, for which—oh God—I would be
ready to climb the steps and fight the boxes
with only nothing, a pair of shoes, and once
inside to open the window and let the snow in
and when the fire was over climb down the icy
fire escape and drop the last twenty
feet with notebooks against my chest, bruises
down one side of my body, fresh blood down the other.

The diction of the poem is an imitation of offhand, rambling speech. Syntactic connections are loose and misleading. The referent of the phrase "for which" in line two is evidently "getting rid of glut" in line one. But the referent of "for which" in line six is not to be found, nor is the referent of the same phrase in the following line. Both are used as repetitive connectors pushing the narrative forward without concern for causality. The described details are likewise obscure, though they seem to represent a dwelling in a state of great disarray, catching fire in the midst of winter and affording the narrator a precarious egress (thanks to his remarkable fitness) via the fire escape. He emerges banged up and bleeding but with his notebooks intact. Such pleasure as there is in this poem comes from its imitation of a tall tale in the style of an insistent but rather spaced-out raconteur. A diligent reader may see the poem as a testament to the value of words or poems (the notebooks) amid the rubble and chaos of disordered life, and the heroic measures needed to preserve them.

I have just cited a currently popular style of which there are many variants. But there is another way to make surreal details speak in a poem, an approach as old as religious mysticism but still capable of considerable power. Handled properly, it promotes a kind of hyperawareness, a multidimensional way of seeing. Here is Edgar Bowers's poem "The Mirror":

Father, I loved you as a child, and still,
When trouble bruises him I can retrace
Back to the time I cannot know, I fill,

By my desire, the possible with grace,
And wait your coming. Then I see my face,
Breathed by some other presence on the chill
Illumination of this mortal glass,
Gleam from the dark and struggle in your will.

In that fixed place, around me, others move,
Vivid with long conclusion, who, once dead,
Quickened the little moment I could prove;
And, though I seem to live, there at my head,
As if the thought translating all I see,
He stands, who was my future, claiming me.

The poem is an address to a God no longer quite believed in, but still treated as a possibility. In that state of mind the poet sees himself as if from the outside, surrounded by many who have gone before him and have helped to form him. Unmoored from time, he recognizes his present vitality as an illusion. In this state of hyper-reality he is already one of the dead, a figure in a procession of the dead, who claims and subsumes the mere momentary troubled individual staring into the mirror. The counterfactual elements in the poem can be readily identified; together they conspire to validate the interpretation I have just given (or one much like it) and, enhanced by the solemnity of the poem's regular meter and rhyme scheme, contribute to its moving and slightly eerie eloquence.

I intend all of these examples to illustrate ways of controlling the progression of thought in a poem rather than to indicate the range or types of ideas that a poet may introduce. But of course the matters are related, for the ingenuity of a poem's juxtaposed details may be a primary source of its attraction, whether those details serve as guideposts directing the poem into new paths or merely as momentary opportunities for depth and insight. It is here that Langer's comments become useful, as she calls attention to "the aura of association of the words, the long or short sequences of ideas, the wealth or poverty of transient imagery that contains them." It is well understood that some poets specialize in ingenious and exotic imagery, while others remain committed to what is sometimes called the plain style.[9]

Still, the question remains whether it is possible to construct a poem entirely out of overtones, out of the *associations* of words rather than their primary meanings. Or, as Davie put it, "to articulate without asserting, to talk without saying what one is talking about." Such a poem, whose course is directed by the auras of its words rather than by their literal or even metaphorical meanings, might constitute an eighth element in our typology. It might be best exemplified by John Ashbery's "Like a Sentence." The poem is longish. I quote the first half:

> How little we know,
> and when we know it!
>
> It was prettily said that "No man
> hath an abundance of cows on the plain, nor shards
> in his cupboard." Wait! I think I know who said that! It was . . .
>
> Never mind, dears, the afternoon
> will fold you up, along with preoccupations
> that now seem so important, until only a child
> running around on a unicycle occupies center stage.
> Then what will you make of walls? And I fear you
> will have to come up with something,
>
> be it a terraced gambit above the sea
> or gossip overheard in the marketplace.
> For you see, it becomes you to be chastened:
> for the old to envy the young,
> and for youth to fear not getting older,
> where the paths through the elms, the carnivals, begin.

After the first two lines we are invited (tempted, challenged?) to add a conclusion to the unfinished sentence before the exclamation mark: "How little we know, / and when we know it . . ." *It is too late!* In the second section the fictitious saying, looking like folk wisdom, appears to mean that all people live with inadequacy. And in the third section the statement "the afternoon / will fold you up" suggests our lives will end with the close of day. We are beginning to see the poem as dealing with transience and the inevitability of death. Once the stage has been cleared (except for the child on the unicycle—the next generation), in what surroundings will we find ourselves? We will have to come up with something, whether fantastical (a "terraced gambit," whatever that might be) or far-fetched (the gossip of the marketplace). Of such wisps is heaven made. And then, in the speaker's nearest approach to direct statement, we're told it's proper to be chastened, for the old to envy the young, and for youth to fear—not just getting older but also, and even more, *not* doing so, as we begin to stray among trees and our imagined entertainments.

Once a few suggestions have been put into the mind, many of the madcap details in the poem support them. By the last section the language comes to achieve a certain eloquence.

> The meter will be screamingly clear then,
> the rhythms unbounced, for though we came
> to life as to a school, we must leave it without graduating
> even as an ominous wind puffs out the sails
> of proud feluccas who don't know where they're headed,
> only that a motion is etched there, shaking to be free.

Death, which has never been mentioned, is by now treated unmistakably in two metaphors: first as leaving (but not graduating from) a school of life, and second as the "ominous wind" filling the sails of the small boats that "don't know where they're headed." And now we see that the *sentence* of the poem's title is in fact the death sentence we all carry. Without employing any of the sequential conventions (consistency of reference, temporal or logical order) that writers ordinarily use to communicate ideas, Ashbery has composed a meditation on human finality whose apparent flippancy belies its fundamental seriousness.

To place this discussion in perspective, it should be re-emphasized that a great many poems do not attempt to convey multiple story lines, however much they may rely on figurative language to amplify meaning. It would be a futile exercise to pore through an anthology with the intention of identifying every poem in it as belonging to one or another of the categories I have laid out here. My intention is not to provide a Swiss army knife capable of prying extra layers of meaning out of every poem encountered. None of these strategies resembles the profligate juxtapositions of details used by Pound in the later Cantos. And none quite accounts for what Yvor Winters calls the postsymbolist technique in which certain words in a poem become imbued because of their context with an extended or metaphorical meaning that goes well beyond their ordinary range of reference.[10] That technique, oddly enough, is closely related to the methods I described in Ashbery's writing, but it is used by Stevens and Valéry, the poets Winters cites, more subtly and more sparingly.

Concision has always been the goal of poets: the conveyance of the maximum amount of information in the minimum number of syllables. And not just information: the concurrent aim is to stir a response equal to the importance of the matter being conveyed. What better way to do this than to say several things at once? And what better medium than language itself, a system of symbols whose referents, circumscribed by convention, can yet be multiplied at will? *Sound, tempo, image, aura*—all these features of language are important in poetic composition, but poets are fundamentally artisans of meaning, and it is by the artful manipulation of meaning that poems achieve their most penetrating and far-ranging effects.

NOTES

1. *Philosophy in a New Key,* 2nd ed. (Harvard University Press, 1996), p. 260; author's italics. Langer, a trained musician herself, blurs many of the distinctions between the expressive techniques of music and those of poetry in order to make her point.

2. *Poetry of Diction in English Verse and Articulate Energy* (combined volume, Carcanet, 1992), p. 273; author's italics.

3. Ibid., p. 323.

4. *Collected Works of Paul Valéry,* ed. Jackson Matthews (Princeton University Press, 1958), p. xxiii.

5. The reader who reflects on the operation of the West African proverb "The ax forgets but not the tree" will understand some of these complexities.

6. *Philosophy in a New Key,* p. 66.

7. See, for example, Bart Eeckhout, "Wallace Stevens' 'Earthy Anecdote'; or, How Poetry Must Resist Ecocriticism Almost Successfully," *Comparative American Studies* 7:2 (2009), pp. 173–92. I have not seen any recognition by commentators that one meaning of "buck" is "the body of a cart or wagon" (OED); cf. "buckboard," a vehicle in common use in nineteenth-century America.

8. Introduced in Tolson's book-length *Harlem Gallery: Raymond Nelson,* ed., *"Harlem Gallery" and Other Poems of Melvin B. Tolson* (Virginia University Press, 1999). The poem is quoted in full in "The Curator as Oracle" below.

9. In an essay called "Looking for Dragon Smoke," Robert Bly makes a case for what he calls freedom of association, by which he means a wide play of imagination in connecting ordinarily distant meanings. Citing his admiration for poets like Blake, Novalis, and Hölderlin, he laments that "passionate association is not to be found in the work of Eliot, Pound, or Williams," and he

observes perceptively that Pound "does not go by secret paths of the imagination—he does it [i.e. makes associations] primarily by juxtaposition of texts; he simply abuts one anecdote to another or one fact to another." *Naked Poetry,* ed. Stephen Berg and Robert Mezey (Bobbs-Merrill, 1969), pp. 162–63.

10. See Yvor Winters, *Forms of Discovery* (Swallow, 1967), pp. 251ff.; especially the discussion on p. 276.

3

THE ELUSIVE SELF
Poems and Personas

"My nerves are bad tonight." Who speaks? Voice, or the putative speaker of the sentences claiming our attention, is central to the understanding of any poem. Whether it is to be taken at face value or with a grain of salt, heard as unaffectedly sincere or urbanely ironic, understood to reflect the poet's views or those of a biased or otherwise limited character—all these considerations must play through the reader's mind as the poem unfolds. As a matter for critical attention, voice is notoriously slippery and perhaps for that reason is often slighted, even in close readings. There is not even a consensus on how to describe it.

The poet-scholar Frederick Turner offers some remarks about the contemporary lyric poem that provide a useful jumping-off point for the present discussion: "What do I mean by 'lyric'? The hallmark of lyric as against any other kind of poetry is the presence of the self of the poet. That self is dominant both in the content and in the form of a lyric poem. Lyric is in the first-person singular. Even when a lyric poem does not directly describe or express the emotions of the poet, its point of view is distinctively subjective, marinated with the poet's feelings and intentions."[1] This is indeed one kind of short poem, and it certainly offers a marked contrast with both the length and the emotional focus of the epic or long narrative poem, with which much of Turner's essay is concerned. But if lyric is in the first-person singular and its hallmark is the presence of the self of the poet, then lyric, so defined, represents only a fraction of the short poems being written in our time. We have come far enough from the days of Percy Shelley, Elizabeth Barrett Browning, and Sara Teasdale that it behooves us to take stock of the short poem in our own day, to see whether we can describe its various voices and the fictions they bring with them, as an aid to later critics who may want to explore one or another category more thoroughly.

As Turner suggests, a grammatical taxonomy offers a good basis for proceeding, though it should be recognized at the outset that, as with the Christian trinity, the three grammatical persons can coexist in the same poem. It makes analytic sense to discuss them individually, but of course it is often from their interaction that fictions are constructed, voices emerge, and poems acquire vitality.

Our notion of the romantic lyric in the first person remains remarkably persistent, even though to find a pure example we have to go back to poets like Teasdale:

Like barley bending
And rising again,
So would I, unbroken,
Rise from pain;

So would I softly,
Day long, night long,
Change my sorrow
Into song.

    —"Like Barley Bending"

But even during Teasdale's time a new generation of poets, both female and male, was changing the nature of the short poem radically. In the hands of writers like Edna St. Vincent Millay and Louise Bogan, the first person lost its aura of naïve sincerity. Two generations later, used by Robert Lowell, Anne Sexton, and Sylvia Plath, it became associated with a desperate and precarious grip on sanity. In Plath's case the ironies included a self-conscious self-advertisement, a far cry from the poems of earlier writers, whose work (as in E. A. Robinson's "Eros Turannos" or T. S. Eliot's "Hysteria") often mimed an overheard personal crisis.

Dying
Is an art, like everything else.
I do it exceptionally well.

I do it so it feels like hell.
I do it so it feels real.
I guess you could say I've a call.

—"Lady Lazarus"

In Sexton's work the anguish is often even more personal and more desperate:

I have known a crib. I have known the tuck-in of a child
but inside my hair waits the night I was defiled.

—"Angel of Clean Sheets"

It is from this complex of tones and voices that we derive our concept of the romantic lyric, the mode in which the feelings of the poet suffuse the poem, passing straight to the reader by a sort of intravenous drip. In our time such poems are less common, and they are often couched in free verse, but variants of them are not hard to find. Here is a passage from "The Knowing" by Sharon Olds, employing her characteristic hydraulics and graced with a most curious simile at the end:

If we
are on our backs, side by side,
with our faces turned fully to face each other,
I can hear a tear from my lower eye
hit the sheet, as if it is an early day on earth,
and then the upper eye's tears
braid and sluice down through the lower eyebrow
like the invention of farming, irrigation, a non-nomadic people.

Poets of course may use the first person in a less romantic but still autobiographical mode, in which the self, rather than serving as the wellspring of constantly changing feeling, is merely a focal point for reflection and commentary, as in Robert Lowell's "For the Union Dead" or Philip Larkin's "Church Going." Sometimes the line between these two modes—reflection and self-absorption—is hazy, as in many of Robert Frost's poems.

They cannot scare me with their empty spaces
Between stars—on stars where no human race is.
I have it in me so much nearer home
To scare myself with my own desert places.

    —"Desert Places"

In other modes, however, the first person represents a persona, a figure who might or might not be the poet and who is there merely to get the action started:

As I walked out one evening,
    Walking down Bristol Street,
The crowds upon the pavement
    Were fields of harvest wheat.

    —W. H. Auden, "As I Walked Out One Evening"

Up from the bronze I saw
Water without a flaw
Rush to its rest in air,
Reach to its rest, and fall.

    —Louise Bogan, "Roman Fountain"[2]

In still others it represents a clearly fictional character:

I have old women's secrets now
That had those of the young;
Madge tells me what I dared not think
When my blood was strong,
And what had drowned a lover once
Sounds like an old song.

    —W. B. Yeats, "The Secrets of the Old"

Here the emotional focus of the poems departs from the intense subjectivity typically associated with what we might call the naïve or unfiltered first-person lyric. The Auden poem turns into a sardonic meditation on time's devastations,

Bogan's becomes a reflection on craft and artistry, and Yeats's fictional portrait derives its force not from feelings claimed by its author but from those of his invented character. An entire genre, the dramatic monologue, is built around the invented character whose narrative constructs a world in itself.[3] Of course an invented character inevitably shares some aspects of its author's psyche and attitude, but the fiction allows for layers of irony between poet and character and thus gives readers leave to scrutinize the evident emotions with greater dispassion, just as Yeats's old woman views love from a nostalgic remove.

. . . .

The appearance of the first-person plural in a poem suggests the idea of a community—either large and generalized or smaller and localized. Traditionally, the large community was humanity in general, addressing a deity: *Laudamus te, benedicimus te, adoramus te, glorificamus te.* Such addresses are less common nowadays, and when we see them they are apt to be short on humility and tinged with irony, as in Gwendolyn Brooks's admonition:

> If Thou be more than hate or atmosphere
> Step forth in splendor, mortify our wolves,
> Or we assume a sovereignty ourselves.

> —Gwendolyn Brooks, "God Works in a Mysterious Way"

More often the community is one that immediately surrounds the mortal subject of the poem:

> The time you won your town the race
> We chaired you through the market-place;
> Man and boy stood cheering by,
> And home we brought you shoulder-high.

> To-day, the road all runners come,
> Shoulder-high we bring you home,
> And set you at your threshold down,
> Townsman of a stiller town.

> —A. E. Housman, "To an Athlete Dying Young"

Or the collective is simply a few people, a convenience for the poet who needs a more impersonal way of contrasting another view with the poem's central focus:

> Whose spirit is this? we said, because we knew
> It was the spirit that we sought and knew
> That we should ask this often as she sang.
>
> —Wallace Stevens, "The Idea of Order at Key West"

In short, the statements uttered in the first-person plural purport to reflect thoughts of a community and to be of general application, although they are technically fictions. Even when the poet goes out of his way to stress the limitations of his chorus's understanding, as Robinson does in the last part of "Eros Turannos," he may invest their words with a lapidary profundity and force:

> Meanwhile we do no harm; for they
>   That with a god have striven,
> Not hearing much of what we say,
>   Take what the god has given;
> Though like waves breaking it may be,
> Or like a changed familiar tree,
> Or like a stairway to the sea
>   Where down the blind are driven.

. . . .

Poems set in the second person often make heavy use of the imperative. They may purport to offer advice (as in Keats's "Ode on Melancholy" or Bogan's "Exhortation") while actually making a statement about the human condition:

> Know once for all: their snare is set
> Even now; be sure their trap is laid;
> And you will see your lifetime yet
> Come to their terms, your plans unmade,—
> And be belied, and be betrayed.
>
> —Bogan, "Exhortation"

39

Still others (though relatively few) attempt to present an entire sequence of events or to draw a portrait using only the second-person singular:

> You write that you are ill, confused. The trees
> Outside the window of the room they gave you
> Are wet with tears each morning when they wake you
> Out of the sleep you never quite fell into.
>
> —Donald Justice, "A Letter"

Occasionally a poem is set in the second person to upbraid or deliver a moral lecture:

> On everything you try
> You take the odds; and chance,
> That mathematic lie,
> Is factored in your glance
> To symbol, perfect fact!
> Till living men, your foes,
> Freeze in your ruthless act:
> They are the pawns you chose.
>
> —Kenneth Fields, "The Game Theorist"

In all these cases the speaker of the poem remains veiled, as it were, a neutral and seemingly objective presence indistinguishable from the poet. What matters about the voice is not the speaker but the relationship its object implies.

Yet frequently a poem turns on the more-or-less equal relation between "I" and "you"—two equal characters in a drama. Peter Dale's "The Terms" provides an excellent example:

> If I should suddenly hear that you were ill
> your letter would have taken a day to come.
> You might be dead before I had the mail
> or die the day I travelled to your room.

And if I were unexpectedly taken ill,
I would not write and trouble you to come
because I know you couldn't help, nor fail
to worry in your dark and curtained room.

This is our friendship. . . .

The second person, we see, is well suited to an intimate dialogue with a fictitious interlocutor ("you") who might need admonition or reproof, as in some
of the examples above, or who might even be a part of oneself and thus in need
of what we might call malign neglect:

And now you're ready who while she was here
Hung like a flag in a calm. Friend, though you stand
Erect and eager, in your eye a tear,
I will not pity you, or lend a hand.

    —J. V. Cunningham

For reasons beyond the grammatical identity between the second persons singular and plural in English, we rarely find poems addressed explicitly to a plural
"you." Richard Wilbur managed it once, in his poem "For the Student Strikers":

Go talk with those who are rumored to be unlike you,
And whom, it is said, you are so unlike.
Stand on the stoops of their houses and tell them why
You are out on strike.

The effect is almost always to place the speaker in a relation of moral superi-
ority to the group addressed, a stance that may impede the poem's reception,
as it did when this poem was written and, as Wilbur testifies, was thrown in
the wastebasket by those who received it.[4]

• • • •

Readers will have noticed that third-person statements figure prominently in
the types of poems we have already discussed. Whether treating agreed-upon

reality or acknowledged fiction, such statements of ostensible fact can hardly be avoided. In poems where they predominate, they quickly establish the fictional terms on which the poem will be understood.

> General Fatigue stalked in, & a Major-General,
> Captain Fatigue, and at the base of all
> pale Corporal Fatigue,
> and curious microbes came, came viruses:
> and the Court conferred on Henry, and conferred on Henry
> the rare Order of Weak.
>
> —John Berryman, "Dream Song 93"

If a poem offers an invented character presented in the third person, that character is often a likely stand-in for the poet, as are all the named figures in the lines just quoted, or the unnamed figure in Robert Frost's "The Most of It":

> He thought he kept the universe alone;
> For all the voice in answer he could wake
> Was but the mocking echo of his own
> From some tree-hidden cliff across the lake.

But many things populate a poem, both concrete and abstract, and at times one may morph into another, as in the same poem, where "the embodiment" of nature's response to the man proves not to be human but rather

> As a great buck it powerfully appeared,
> Pushing the crumpled water up ahead,
> And landed pouring like a waterfall,
> And stumbled through the rocks with horny tread,
> And forced the underbrush—and that was all.

Such a fictional strategy carries us far from the romantic impulse of the traditional lyric, which might have railed against nature in the first person, in a voice like Ahab's or Lear's, demanding a response from the impersonal elements. Here, deprived of the scope of a tragic play or novel, both poets—

Berryman and Frost—rely on the irony implicit in a third-person depiction of both the anguished narcissist and the natural world's response.[5]

Frost doubtless speaks for many poets when he explains the fictionalizing impulse in "Build Soil":

Life may be tragically bad, and I
Make bold to sing it so, but do I dare
Name names and tell you who by name is wicked?
. . . .
I prefer to sing safely in the realm
Of types, composite and imagined people:
To affirm there is such a thing as evil
Personified, but ask to be excused
From saying on a jury "Here's the guilty."

So a great number of poems—and not just by Frost—are peopled with invented characters, fancifully named (as in Berryman's poem) or unnamed, along with natural objects of all sorts, emotions, abstract concepts, and miscellaneous animals. It is even possible, as Carolyn Kizer demonstrates, to turn a portion of one's personality into a four-legged creature:

Now, when he and I meet, after all these years,
I say to the bitch inside me, don't start growling.
He isn't a trespasser anymore,
Just an old acquaintance tipping his hat.
My voice says, "Nice to see you,"
As the bitch starts to bark hysterically.
He isn't an enemy now,
Where are your manners, I say . . .

    —"Bitch"

And not to be ignored is the descriptive essay presented entirely in the third person, with the same objectivity one might find in a piece of fiction. Here is Thom Gunn's description of two down-and-out men on an obscure city street:

>   . . . times are
> he sleeps it off across the back seat
> of an auto with four flat tyres,
> blackened sole and heel
> jammed against the side windows,
> bearded face blinded by sleep
> turned toward the light.
> Another lies on the front seat.
>
> A poor weed,
> unwanted scraggle tufted
> with unlovely yellow,
> persists between paving stones
> marginal to the grid
> bearded face turned toward light.
>
>   —"Outside the Diner"

It is easy enough in such poems for the poet, or speaking voice, to intrude and direct the reader's response, much as a television cameraman will use a reaction shot of the host during an interview, and many poets indeed do this. But, as this poem demonstrates, the careful selection of details, without recourse to any first-person statement, can accomplish the same objective.

Then there are poems, or passages of poems, that seek a measure of distance by resorting to the impersonal "one" in lieu of the first person—a mannerism Americans tend to associate with British speakers of a certain type or class. Wallace Stevens, a writer who never left American soil, uses this form in "The Man Whose Pharynx Was Bad." The poem's first stanza, employing the ingenuous first person, recalls the old lyric mode in which the poet's feelings and responses take center stage: "Mildew of summer and the deepening snow / Are both alike in the routine I know."[6] It concludes with memorable awkwardness, "I am too dumbly in my being pent." But the latter half of the poem, growing at once more meditative and more cautious, moves into the objective third person. Perhaps, it says, if winter could penetrate to "the final slate,"

> One might in turn become less diffident,
> Out of such mildew plucking neater mould

And spouting new orations of the cold.
One might. One might. But time will not relent.

The poem can be seen as a deliberate attempt to wrench the poet's sensibility out of the self-obsession implied by the first-person complaint and force it
into a greater objectivity—verbal at least if not yet convincingly psychological.

In fact, one of the interesting psychological phenomena to be discerned in
contemporary short poetry is what might be called the masked emotion: an
evocation of mood, attitude, or state of mind that is pervasive but not ascribed
to an identifiable person. The tonality is lyric, but the voice is resolutely in the
third person, as in this poem by Philip Larkin:

Cut grass lies frail:
Brief is the breath
Mown stalks exhale.
Long, long the death

It dies in the white hours
Of young-leafed June
With chestnut flowers,
With hedges snowlike strewn,

White lilac bowed,
Lost lanes of Queen Anne's lace
And that high-builded cloud
Moving at summer's pace.

—"Cut Grass"

This seems a largely successful attempt to recreate the intense focus and feeling
of romantic poetry, of a type often centered on natural phenomena. It treads, I
would say, perilously close to the pathetic fallacy but does so without exposing
a self whose personality some would consider irrelevant to, and distracting
from, the issue at hand—namely a lament for inevitable decline and decay in
the midst of plenty.

All these uses of grammatical persons, singular and plural, are aimed at
constructing fictions by which poets can achieve various degrees of ironic

detachment from the emotionally compelling and often deeply personal material they are working with. To protect their work from being "distinctively subjective," and to avoid subject matter "marinated with the poet's feelings and intentions," they develop characters that are not themselves and create situations that cannot be confused with their own, save by the most perverse interpreters.

There is a final type of objective, third-person statement, seldom discussed, that stands outside the fictional context in which most poems are presented. It is the statement with a universal noun as subject and a verb in the absolute present, rendering by that means a verdict not on the particular fictional world of the poem but on the universe in general: the one we all inhabit. It thus invites the reader to judge its truth without the usual contextual qualifications.

In her quirky poem "He 'Digesteth Harde Yron,'" Marianne Moore talks of the aepyornis, the roc, and the moa by way of introducing what the ancient Egyptians called the camel-sparrow, which we know as the ostrich. Seven stanzas discuss legends, lore, and ostensible facts about the bird in a manner suggesting we need not give any of this too much credence. Then comes the eighth stanza, with its opening line: "The power of the visible is the invisible." The sphere of application of that sentence extends far outside the poem: it is a comment on things in general. That it may not be altogether plain on first encounter does not reduce its universality or its air of authority. Such statements are nearly always memorable, and they tend to become aphorisms.

Consider some other well-known examples:

No ideas but in things.

Man is the intelligence of his soil.

The expense of spirit in a waste of shame
Is lust in action . . .

Nothing gold can stay.

Parting is all we know of heaven
And all we need of hell.

Smiles are for youth. For old age come
Death's terror and oblivion.[7]

Such statements, by their rarity and their surprisingly emphatic tone, tend to stay in our minds, even if—as in some of the cases above—we may have trouble decoding their precise meaning. They move the poem at least temporarily out of the territory of fiction and into the realm of philosophy, where assertions are made about the nature of things.

Though the short poem largely, but by no means entirely, eschews the narrative poem's techniques for developing events and characters over time, it regularly deploys many other resources of narrative, including the creation of characters, often with distinctive voices, the playing of one character against another, and the projection, through their voices (or that of the poem's ostensible speaker), of finely controlled levels of irony. Stepping through the grammatical persons associated with these voices has allowed us to survey these resources and mark off some boundaries between them. It has also demonstrated the wide variety of tones, characters, and associated subjects at play in poems written in the last century and the present one—a variety for which the term "lyric" in its usual understanding is quite inadequate. Critics still face the daunting task of analyzing the kinds and degrees of irony that qualify the voices we've been surveying. Doing so will help to show how poets are able to gain and maintain distance on their experiences and the feelings that accompany them—not to denature or desiccate their lines but to empower and universalize them.

NOTES

1. Frederick Turner, "Lyric and the Content of Poetry," *Think Journal*, 5:2 (2015), p. 69.

2. The near exclusion of self was quite deliberate. While the poem was still in flux, Bogan wrote to Rolfe Humphries, "It should be all fountain, and no Louise looking at it" (July 2, 1935, quoted in *A Poet's Prose*, ed. Mary Kinzie [Swallow, 2005]).

3. Chapter 13 gives examples.

4. Wilbur's notes (*Collected Poems, 1943–2004* [Harcourt, 2004], p. 189) add that the poem was later retrieved and published. For another example of a speaker addressing an audience to whom he stands in a morally superior relation, consider the speech of Thomas More in a passage of the Elizabethan drama *Sir Thomas More* attributed to Shakespeare:

> Imagine that you see the wretched strangers,
> Their babies at their backs and their poor luggage,
> Plodding to th' ports and coasts for transportation,
> And that you sit as kings in your desires,
> Authority quite silent by your brawl,

And you in ruff of your opinions clothed;
What had you got? I'll tell you: you had taught
How insolence and strong hand should prevail,
How order should be quelled; and by this pattern
Not one of you should live an aged man . . .

5. I pass over Frost's many narrative poems with well-defined characters, such as "The Death of the Hired Man" and "Home Burial," because they fall outside the purview of short poems I have adopted for this discussion. But it is not hard to find poems not longer than a sestina with defined characters (presented in the third person) who interact with each other.

6. A common romantic complaint at the time, evidently. T. S. Eliot has Prufrock say, "I have measured out my life with coffee spoons."

7. The quotations are, of course, respectively from Williams, Stevens, Shakespeare, Frost, Dickinson, and Larkin.

4

BUT ENOUGH ABOUT ME
Poems without Personas

O wad some Power the giftie gie us
To see oursels as ithers see us!
It wad frae mony a blunder free us,
An' foolish notion.

    —Robert Burns

Sara Teasdale, Vachel Lindsay, Hart Crane, Sylvia Plath, Anne Sexton, John Berryman, Richard Brautigan—diverse as these writers were, they all died by their own hand.[1] In the general American population the suicide rate is approximately 13 in 100,000. If there were 50,000 poets of major reputation in the country during the decades when these people lived and died, we might say their suicides did not exceed the norm; but there were not. Therefore we must conclude that at some point in our history suicide became an occupational hazard of the poetic vocation. To be sure, there were extenuating circumstances: alcoholism, abusive childhoods, disappointments in love, and betrayal by loved ones. But these misfortunes occur in many other lives as well. It is reasonable to ask if there is something in the act of writing poetry—or the disposition to write it—that puts the writer in particular danger. The ancient Chinese evidently thought so. Don Paterson gives us a version of a short poem by Li Po about a colleague:

> I found him wandering on the hill
> one hot blue afternoon.

He looked as skinny as a nail,
as pale-skinned as the moon;

below the broad shade of his hat
his face was cut with rain.
Dear God, poor Du Fu, I thought:
It's the poetry again.

    —"The Poetry"

So what is it about "the poetry"—and particularly about the poetry of the twentieth century—that endangers its practitioners the way the song "Gloomy Sunday" reputedly endangered all who heard it?[2] A definitive answer to that question may never be found, but if we're alert we can see poets here and there casting about for a protective talisman. Louise Bogan, who knew something about seasons in hell, having spent several extended periods in psychiatric hospitals recovering from breakdowns, saw that it was somehow important that writers remain separate from their writing. She wrote in "To an Artist, to Take Heart":

Slipping in blood, by his own hand, through pride,
Hamlet, Othello, Coriolanus fall.
Upon his bed, however, Shakespeare died,
Having endured them all.

She was not often heeded. John Berryman, who spent years maintaining to everyone who asked that the Henry of the *Dream Songs* was not himself, knew also that Henry was his stand-in. In a telling moment in his *Paris Review* interview, he stumbled in his attempt to keep his real and his fictional selves separate:

Berryman: It did not occur to me to have a dialogue between them—to insert bodily Henry into the poem . . . *Me,* to insert me, in my own person, John Berryman, *I,* into the poem . . .

Interviewer: Was that a Freudian slip?

Berryman: I don't know. Probably.[3]

Later in the same interview, talking of the composition of *Love & Fame*, he seemed to give up on the aspiration to write objectively: "The subject on which I am a real authority is me, so I wiped out all the disguises and went to work."

Leaving aside the question whether one is ever a real authority on oneself (see this essay's epigraph), a poet might ponder whether it is possible to become too obsessed with his or her own responses to the slings and arrows that pelt us all. That is not a dubiety foremost in every poet's mind; nevertheless, some are (or appear to be) endowed with a certain reticence that steers them away from both confession and self-obsession. Such poets often make strenuous efforts to avoid tapping too quickly into the wellsprings of their own feelings. They may even evince a reflexive suspicion of first-person grammatical forms, the mode of discourse so natural to the lyric poet as to seem all but unavoidable.

There are of course many ways to write a poem in the first person while still guarding against public exposure. One can adopt a straightforward reportorial style, as if relating one's own perceptions as they might be seen by somebody else. One can pretend to *be* somebody else, with an eccentric background and a clearly limited or biased view of the world. One can begin a narrative in the first person but continue in the third, as if a trusted witness were narrating only objective facts. Or one can adopt a naïve tone, creating a persona who seems more innocent or unaware than the poet herself. ("What's wrong about self-pity anyway?" asks Elizabeth Bishop's Robinson Crusoe.)[4]

All these devices are ways of bringing color, which is to say feeling, into a poem. They work well because readers quickly infer the emotional force behind a first-person statement, even one that purports not to be the poet's own. It's a faculty we all need to function in a social world. But a poet who distrusts the ease of thus enlisting the reader as an emotional ally, who wants to ensure that no unjustified or too readily intuited feeling can creep into a poem, may choose to rule out first-person narrative altogether and attempt to generate any and all sympathies only through the careful assembly and declamation of artfully chosen facts. Such an approach—employing what we might call scrupulous objectivity—poses special challenges for the writer. I mean to explore several varieties of this cultivated neutrality here.

No Ideas but in Things
If the poem deals with inanimate matter, its human meaning must be communicated without an ostensible narrator to react to it. One way to do that is

THE CONTENT OF POETRY

through tone. Kay Ryan, for example, generally avoids creating an identifiable persona but still writes in a voice that might belong to a friend or neighbor to comment and direct our attention to her subject's human relevance:

A Plain Ordinary Steel Needle Can Float on Pure Water

    —Ripley's Believe It or Not

Who hasn't seen
a plain ordinary
steel needle float serene
on water as if lying on a pillow?
The water cuddles up like Jell-O.
It's a treat to see water
so rubbery, a needle
so peaceful, the point encased
in the tenderest dimple.
It seems so *simple*
when things or people
have modified each other's qualities
somewhat;
we almost forget the oddity
of that.

There's a peculiar kind of alchemy afoot in this poem. The authorial voice, seemingly a fount of common sense, makes an unwarranted inference in order to draw a human moral from the observed facts. The objects in question—needle and water—have not modified each other's qualities but have merely taken advantage of one of water's less apparent features, its surface tension, to produce a counter-intuitive spectacle. By infusing her narration with a tone of quiet conviction and wry astonishment, the poet carries off her subtle deception, and in the process makes a keen point about human psychology, without need for a distinct narrative persona.

If the subject is animate, nonhuman nature, the writer can seek to avoid lending it human-like qualities that would risk sentimentalizing it. Yet there must be an emotional connection, and the human resemblance cannot be entirely suppressed. Sometimes it is suggested quite indirectly. Consider Emily Dickinson's well-known poem "Further in Summer Than the Birds." Written strictly in the third person, the poem relies on statements that purport to describe a scene in nature through metaphor.

Further in summer than the Birds—
Pathetic from the grass—
A minor Nation celebrates
Its unobtrusive Mass.

No Ordinance be seen—
So gradual the Grace,
A gentle Custom it becomes—
Enlarging Loneliness—

Antiquest felt at Noon—
When August burning low
Arise this spectral Canticle
Repose to typify—

Remit as yet no grace—
No furrow on the Glow,
Yet a Druidic Difference
Enhances Nature now—

We infer that the chirping or buzzing of insects—probably cicadas or crickets—is being likened to a human ritual. The poem offers the reader barely enough concrete detail to determine what is happening, and much of that detail is provided only at a metaphorical level: *nation, mass, ordinance, grace, custom, canticle*. The adjectives lend no more specificity, but qualify the feeling the poet wants to convey: *pathetic, minor, unobtrusive, gentle, spectral, druidic*. In short, because the poem is seeking to explain why a natural phenomenon can evoke such strong feeling, Dickinson relies heavily on quasi-religious metaphor and on adjectives that would likely not be found in the prose of an entomologist. In doing so she scants the obligation to help readers see or hear what she is talking about (in fact the physical details of her subject appear not to interest her greatly), but compensates by creating a lush and memorable emotional aura.

We have, it would seem, much to learn from the insect world. Employing a similar strategy in "How to Paint a Water Lily," Ted Hughes declines to engage personally with his subject, instead adopting the tone of a guidebook or instruction manual to describe essentially human matters in terms of the inhuman other:

> First observe the air's dragonfly
> That eats meat, that bullets by
> Or stands in space to take aim;
> Others as dangerous comb the hum
> Under the trees. There are battle-shouts
> And death-cries everywhere hereabouts
> But inaudible, so the eyes praise
> To see the colours of these flies
> Rainbow their arcs, spark, or settle
> Cooling like beads of molten metal
> Through the spectrum.

The menace so often observed in Hughes's poems is palpable here. What was a religious ritual in Dickinson becomes a microcosmic war here, contributing to the unnerving conclusion that beauty and terror in life are at some deep level inseparable.

By contrast, here's a rather more benign poem by Philip Larkin, called "Pigeons":

> On shallow slates the pigeons shift together,
> Backing against a thin rain from the west
> Blown across each sunk head and settled feather.
> Huddling round the warm stack suits them best,
> Till winter daylight weakens, and they grow
> Hardly defined against the brickwork. Soon,
> Light from a small intense lopsided moon
> Shows them, black as their shadows, sleeping so.

The poem is part of an ongoing project discernible in Larkin's work: to write straightforward description without the insertion of an ostensible sensibility conferred by a persona, while yet allowing mood, perspective, and feeling to emerge as it were from the details alone. It is a dignified poem that successfully evokes feelings of somber pity for weak creatures in an indifferent landscape, even while it eschews both the implied violence of Hughes's world and the mystical associations Dickinson conjures with her highly allusive metaphorical language.

If the subject is the interactions among people, the writer becomes a dramatist who deals with the struggles of others—a rewarding but challenging role to accomplish in the compass of a brief poem. Most of Robert Frost's efforts in this form approach the length of a prose short story. To achieve condensation the poet must generalize. In "The Darkness and the Light Are Both Alike to Thee," Anthony Hecht views his human subjects from a great distance, not mentioning them until halfway through the poem. The third-person narration makes human beings seem secondary to the points of light that outlast the darkness but fade in daylight. Thus the true emotional focus of the poem is treated almost as an afterthought.

> Distantly lights go on.
> Scattered like fallen sparks
> Bedded in peat, they seem
> Set in the plushest darks
> Until a timid gleam
> Of matins turns them wan,
>
> Like the elderly and frail
> Who've lasted through the night,
> Cold brows and silent lips,
> For whom the rising light
> Entails their own eclipse,
> Brightening as they fail.

Instead of pity for nonhuman creatures with whose physical needs we can empathize, we are asked here to pity frail human beings at the end of life, who recognize in the ascendant morning their own extinguishment. The notion that "life goes on" is small comfort to those for whom it does not. By locating a large theme in an ordinary diurnal event, Hecht is able to write movingly and impersonally at the same time.

Retreat from the Concrete

Another way out of the cage of the first person, a way rarely explored in our day, is through pure abstraction: the statement and defense in verse of a philosophical position—often one with strong moral implications—that the poet associates not with himself personally but with mankind in general. Such statements were frequent among Elizabethan writers. In his "Chorus Sacerdotum," Fulke Greville lamented,

> Is it the mark, or majesty of power
> To make offences that it may forgive?
> Nature herself, doth her own self deflower,
> To hate those errors she herself doth give.

And Shakespeare treated one aspect of nature's ambiguous generosity in highly stylized rhetoric in Sonnet 129: "The expense of spirit in a waste of shame / Is lust in action . . ."

But rare are the twentieth-century poets who have followed suit. T. S. Eliot stated abstract truths some might consider obvious in the opening lines of "Burnt Norton":

> Time present and time past
> Are both perhaps present in time future
> And time future contained in time past.
> If all time is eternally present
> All time is unredeemable.
> What might have been is an abstraction
> Remaining a perpetual possibility
> Only in a world of speculation.

Making such arguments, convincing or otherwise, used to be one of the things poems could do. Extensions of this way of writing in abstractions were occasionally tried out in later decades, notably by some students of Yvor Winters. Thom Gunn, for example, employs the abstract style occasionally, as in his poem "Berlin in Ruins," in which he meditates on the Anhalter Bahnhof, now a mere shell of the once massive building:

> The mind does not rest without peril
> among the tarnished blades of laurel:
>
> it may cut on them, it may fester
> —until it throbs with a revived fear
> of the dark hysteric conqueror
>
> returning from France in triumph as
> the hectic that overtakes process,
> beneath a silk tent of swastikas.
>
> And fever may descend on the brow
> like the high circlet, in whose shadow
> the mind awakes, bathed in poison now;
>
> or, harder and sharper than bronze, still
> supporting the insupportable,
> it may survive its own stiff laurel.

Characteristics of this style are phrases like "the mind," "the brow," and unidiomatic abstractions like "the hectic that overtakes process." Readers may be able to puzzle out meaning and even derive a sense of moral discomfort from a poem of this kind, but the effort takes patience and a willingness to give the poem the benefit of the doubt. Gunn's natural disposition lay elsewhere, and he soon left this style behind.

As did most of his contemporaries. We have made a great collective shift toward the dramatic and the immediate and have all but abandoned abstract statement except in the context of a clearly recognizable dramatic setting. This may be a gain, but it is more likely a sign of the current zeitgeist and destined to change once again. In our present climate, at least one poet, Louise Glück, offers in "The Winged Horse" a tongue-in-cheek confession to a certain nostalgia for a once respectable poetic style:

Here is my horse Abstraction,
silver-white, color of the page,
of the unwritten.

Come, Abstraction,
by Will out of Demonic Ambition:
carry me lightly into the regions of the immortal.

I am weary of my other mount,
by Instinct out of Reality,
color of dust, of disappointment,

. . .

Then come, Abstraction,
take me where you have taken so many others,
far from here, to the void, the star pasture.

Bear me quickly,
Dream out of Blind Hope.

Glück, of course, does establish a persona in this poem, one that operates behind a screen of irony that is fully consistent with the wry self-critical and skep-
tical stance she adopts even in the midst of her most intense self-analysis. That
too is a form of protective firewall.

Myth

Glück's horse, Abstraction, is modeled on mythical horses such as Pegasus, that
possess supernatural powers, and in that respect her poem points to another
ancient objectifying technique, the narrative of classical myth. Even though
familiarity with the details of ancient myth can no longer be assumed in a lit-
erate audience, the technique can be an effective way to present emotionally
complex and sometimes wrenching material without directly implicating the
poet herself. Here, for example, is "Actaeon" by A. E. Stallings:

The hounds, you know them all by name.
You fostered them from purblind whelps
At their dam's teats, and you have come
To know the music of their yelps:

High-strung Anthee, the brindled bitch,
The blue-tick coated Philomel,
And freckled Chloe, who would fetch
A pretty price if you would sell—

All fleet of foot, and swift to scent,
Inexorable once on the track,
Like angry words you might have meant,
But do not mean, and can't take back.

There was a time when you would brag
How they would bay and rend apart
The hopeless belling from a stag.
You falter now for the foundered hart.

Desires you nursed of a winter night—
Did you know then why you bred them—
Whose needling milk-teeth used to bite
The master's hand that leashed and fed them?

To comprehend the poem we are required to know at least the outlines of the myth of Actaeon, the hunter who came across the naked Artemis bathing, and for his trespass was turned into a stag that was then set upon by his own dogs, who tore him limb from limb. The poem lavishes what seems at first like inordinate detail on the hounds, and not so much on Actaeon himself, who is addressed in the second person, like an intimate, or perhaps a self. But then some linguistic sleight of hand changes our perspective. The "hart," a synonym for "stag," might be a pun. And in the last stanza the dogs have become desires, nursed over time and finally capable of consuming their possessor. They are, we learned a few lines back, like angry words that, once turned loose, cannot be recanted. Without directly implicating its author, or any other living soul, the poem stands as a cautionary tale of destructive emotions given too free rein.

Beyond Words

And then there is metaphor—specifically the symbolic treatment of the poet's own problems and dilemmas as though they concerned someone else altogether, someone who lived a far different life from one's own. In "Roman

Fountain," Louise Bogan poses as merely an observer, an "I" who gets the poem started, then stands back and lets the water gush:

> Up from the bronze I saw
> Water without a flaw
> Rush to its rest in air,
> Reach to its rest, and fall.
>
> Bronze of the blackest shade,
> An element man-made,
> Shaping upright the bare
> Clear gouts of water in air.
>
> O, as with arm and hammer,
> Still it is good to strive
> To beat out the image whole,
> To echo the shout and stammer
> When full-gushed waters, alive,
> Strike on the fountain's bowl
> After the air of summer.

Apart from the superb description of the up-rushing water, the point of the poem resides in the last seven lines, which urge the craftsman to "beat out the image whole" in imitation of the fountain so brilliantly evoked. In somewhat the same way, Derek Walcott in "Night Fishing" obliquely discusses the problem of writing poetry without ever mentioning himself or even, specifically, poetry:

> Line, trawl for each word
> with the homesick toss
> of a black pirogue anchored
> in stuttering phosphorus.
>
> The crab-fishers' torches
> keep to the surf's crooked line,
> and a cloud's page scorches
> with a smell of kerosene.

Thorny stars halo
the sybil's black cry:
"*Apotherein thelo*
I am longing to die."

But, line, live in the sounds
that ignorant shallows use;
then throw the silvery nouns
to open-mouthed canoes.

Readers familiar with Walcott's work will recognize here his tendency to treat the entire world as a book in which poems can be read and written. The line between the word and the world is as thin as the letter "l" and as liquid. For our purposes the poem illustrates a way of discussing a matter of central concern to the poet while maintaining an ostensible focus on fishing—the livelihood of Walcott's compatriots and the activity most evocative of life on his native islands.

To forestall objections, let me make it clear that I do not believe a poet must abandon any use of a persona in order to write objectively, to escape the tyranny of the self. There are many forms of disguise, many masks that can be highly effective and endlessly entertaining. But writing in an ostensibly neutral voice, not attributable to anyone in particular, is challenging for a poet who wishes, while doing so, to communicate strong feeling and a sense of immediacy. It is one more self-imposed restriction but one that, brought off successfully, allows the poem a kind of lapidary grandeur that sets it apart from its more importunate fellows.

More than that, it grants the poet (or compels him to achieve) a certain distance from his own personality, with its neuroses and anxieties of the kind Philip Larkin so memorably conveyed, in the first person, in "Aubade." Fictional though that distance may be, it still offers a different sort of lens—and a wide-angle one at that—through which to view his tumultuous times and his equally tumultuous self. Perhaps we should offer the last word, or words, to W. H. Auden, who strove all his life for this kind of objectivity. He came close to it in "Look, Stranger":

Far off like floating seeds the ships
Diverge on urgent voluntary errands;

And the full view
Indeed may enter
And move in memory as now these clouds do,
That pass the harbour mirror
And all the summer through the water saunter.

Like many introspective people, certain poets search for an angle of vision offering an objective view of experience. In that search they encounter, I believe, an especially narrow gate to pass through because they traffic, by profession, in those moments when the nerves are most on edge, when perceptions and feelings are keenest. The search has its rewards, but also its pangs of renunciation. Auden left a memorable record of his struggle in a first-person poem, "The More Loving One":

Were all the stars to disappear or die,
I should learn to look at an empty sky
And feel its total dark sublime,
Though this might take me a little time.

NOTES

1. So, perhaps, did Randall Jarrell, killed by an automobile on the highway during a period of profound depression.

2. In the German-Hungarian film of the same name (German title: "Ein Lied von Liebe und Tod"), those who hear the song often commit suicide, as does its composer.

3. John Berryman, *Paris Review* interview (Winter 1972), "The Art of Poetry," no. 16.

4. Elizabeth Bishop, "Crusoe in England."

5

ALL IN THE FAMILY
Parents and Children in Today's Poetry

One of the most striking features of contemporary poetry is its frequent focus on familial relations—between parents and young children and between middle-aged children and their aging parents. This is new. Previous generations of poets generally skirted the topic. Certainly, many poets treated the death of children (as did Ben Jonson in his moving poem "On My First Son"). But rare are poems dealing with intergenerational relationships. Coleridge in "Frost at Midnight" wrote of his hopes for his infant child; Anne Bradstreet wrote of her children only to describe their flight from the nest; and Elizabeth Barrett Browning wrote poems decrying the mistreatment or exploitation of children, a topic thrust into prominence by the industrial revolution. Yet despite the example of novelists from Austen to Turgenev and Tolstoy, explorations of the nature of affection (or more complicated emotions) between parents and children rarely found their way into English-language poetry before the years following World War II.

There are several possible explanations for this reticence. To a greater extent than many would admit, poets tend to imitate each other. For generations the poetic representation of love followed patterns laid down in the Middle Ages by the traditions of courtly love: the gallant and possibly hopeless pursuit by the male lover of an idealized woman who might or might not yield to him. (One who might desire him on her own initiative was almost certainly up to no good.) Even when, in later times, the sought-after woman became more attainable, her fidelity could not be counted on; the rejected lover became a standard figure.

But all is turned thorough my gentleness
Into a strange fashion of forsaking,
And I have leave to go of her goodness,
And she also to use newfangleness.

    —Thomas Wyatt, "They flee from me"

So strong and enduring were these conventions that when women began to publish poems on a more-or-less equal footing, they often turned their alleged inconstancy into a badge of honor. So Edna St. Vincent Millay admonishes a lover that he will someday be doomed

To walk the world forever for my sake,
And in each chamber find me gone again!

    —Sonnet XII

But these are poems, however stylized, of love between men and women. If frequency of expression is a measure, the feelings of parents for children in earlier generations did not rise to anything like that level of importance in the poetic canon. Why not? One answer could certainly be a bias on the part of the male establishment against subjects thought to be the exclusive province of women. Sabine Durrant tells us that when Sharon Olds first sent her poems to a journal she received a reply saying, "This is a literary magazine. If you wish to write about this sort of subject, may we suggest the *Ladies' Home Journal*. The true subjects of poetry are . . . male subjects, not your children."[1]

But apart from the force of tradition and the dominance of men among widely published poets, was there also a concern that depiction of the tender feelings of parents for children might taint a poem with sentimentality?

We all know sentimentality—as we know pornography—when we see it. Or do we? When Wordsworth writes of an infant in "Intimations of Immortality" is he being sentimental?

See, where 'mid work of his own hand he lies,
Fretted by sallies of his mother's kisses,
With light upon him from his father's eyes!

The poem depicts infancy in a conventional and idealized light, offering no unexpected detail to impress it on the memory. The perspective seems imbued with a deliberate and unrealistic sweetness.

Sentimentality is even easier to spot, we might think, in the stereotypical domestic poems of nineteenth-century America, such as Longfellow's "The Children's Hour." But to what extent is our reaction formed by factors outside the standard definition of sentimentality (emotion exceeding the occasion)—factors such as meter (anapestic) or diction ("the round-tower of my heart," "forever and a day")? In other words, are we perhaps condemning Longfellow and his peers simply for sounding like nineteenth-century poets? Yet it is undeniable that such poems cloy.

Even in the twentieth century the reflexive addition of extra sweetness where children are concerned was a hard habit to break. John Crowe Ransom's much-anthologized poem "Bells for John Whiteside's Daughter" treats a child's death with discretion but still indulges in the courtly condescension of phrases like "the tireless heart within the little / Lady" while displacing much of its sentiment onto the storybook geese that animate the verses.

One of the antidotes to the temptation to dote obsessively on an individual is to universalize, to offer a general rather than a personal statement, or to clothe the particular in metaphor, so that any affective motive is disguised beyond recognition. When Louise Bogan chose to write about her daughter Maidie, she called the poem "M., Singing":

> Now, innocent, within the deep
> Night of all things you turn the key,
> Unloosing what we know in sleep.
> In your fresh voice they cry aloud
> Those beings without heart or name.

The singing "innocent" is here merely a means of releasing the phantasms of the unconscious mind. She (we only guess at the gender) is neither praised nor blamed for this; her relation to the speaker is not at issue in the poem.

Other means of objectifying a fraught relationship include the dramatic monologue (Robert Browning's "My Last Duchess" or "A Woman's Last Word") or the verse portrait in short compass, often implying a relationship, as in

E. A. Robinson's "Reuben Bright" or his longer masterpiece, "Eros Turannos." Robert Frost extended the scope in poems like "Home Burial" to effectively a short-story length. All the poems I've mentioned deal with relations between a man and wife, though in the Frost poem that relation is made radioactive by the parties' feelings about their dead son.

It was with some effort that poets began to write about their feelings for children in a voice that could not be accused of sentimentality. In "Morning Song" Sylvia Plath wrote, contemplating her newborn son:

> I'm no more your mother
> Than the cloud that distills a mirror to reflect its own slow
> Effacement at the wind's hand.

—a rather unclear metaphor designed, one suspects, to ward off imputations of maternal softness.

Sometimes lumped with Plath as a "confessional" poet, Robert Lowell wrote numerous poems that mention family members, particularly his second wife, Elizabeth ("Lizzy"), their daughter Harriet, and his third wife, Caroline. The poems contain vivid moments but tend to focus more on Lowell himself than on his relationship with wife or daughter. The fifth poem in *For Lizzie and Harriet* (called "Harriet") characterizes his daughter as one readying for the title role in *Romeo and Juliet*:

> Child of ten, three-quarters animal,
> three years from Juliet, half Juliet,
> already ripened for the night on stage—
> beautiful petals, what shall we hope for,
> knowing one choice, not two, is all you're given,
> health beyond measure, dangerous
> to yourself, more dangerous to others?

The question mark at the end suggests Lowell's uncertainty about this portrait. Is it an expectation, a hope, or a fear?

The poems I've mentioned were intended to represent experiences familiar to most of their readers. They offered the comfort of acquiescence in a universal truth. But they shed little light on the actual relations between parents and children. In the real world such relations reveal enough complexity and variety that the anatomy of any one of them might well seem strange, or at least offer surprises, to people encountering it through a poem. But to understand it, both poet and reader must move beyond the formulaic.

They were aided in that endeavor by the permeation of Freudian thinking into English and American culture in the years following the Second World War. It was not necessary that writers adopt the schema of Freud's "family romance" as a means of understanding the self; probably most did not. But a general understanding of the individual came to depend, for many writers who had undergone psychoanalysis, on an awareness of family dynamics. As Mark Poster observes,

> The family is the nexus of the experiences with which psychoanalysis is concerned. Freud seeks to decompose the individual into his essential (but unconscious) family relationships. The achievement of psychoanalysis is to unmask the illusion of individualism, of the self-contained, autonomous nature of personal experience and motivation. As an isolated unit, the individual is unintelligible to the analyst. The most personal and particular characteristics of the individual's inner life remain obscure, only becoming meaningful signs when they are traced back to the medically significant body of the family. Hence, the family is the secret of the individual.

And he adds, "The fundamental principle of Freudian psychology is that the structure of the mind is formed in childhood. The mind is not, therefore, pregiven, but built up through a process."[2]

Slowly and with some false starts it became possible for poets to write about their own experience with children (or as children) without suggesting that in so doing they were retelling a universal story. Readers, it turned out, did not reject the resulting poems because of their particularity; instead they discovered elements they could recognize and relate to in details that may or may not have matched their own experience. Theodore Roethke's "My Papa's Waltz" captured the imaginations of many people who had never danced as a child with a dirt-caked, half-drunken father. Elizabeth Bishop's "Sestina" evoked the tedium and suppressed sadness of a rainy afternoon spent by a child with her grandmother before a stove, with only an almanac for distraction. And the frankness and rawness of W. D. Snodgrass's "Heart's Needle" won over a generation of readers who had not seen before a father's portrayal of his grief over the loss of his daughter through divorce:

> Winter again and it is snowing;
> Although you are still three,
> You are already growing
> Strange to me.
>
> . . .
>
> I lift you on your swing and must
>   shove you away,
> see you return again,
> drive you off again, then
>
> stand quiet till you come.
>   You, though you climb
> higher, farther from me, longer,
>   will fall back to me stronger.

These poems broke new ground. They demonstrated that the representation of tender feelings between parents and children did not necessarily result in sentimentality, and that the intensely personal could be universal at the same time without being maudlin. But the question of an appropriate level of feeling still hovered.

"Emotion appropriate to the occasion" seems a simple enough formula, but it becomes complicated and murky when we examine the relations between parents and children. For the emotional connections between them are inherently strong, complex, and often volatile. Who is to say if the emotion aroused by a depiction of a mother nursing her infant, or a father keeping watch over a sick child, is proper to the occasion? Context is everything. The reader (who is inevitably a critic) must ask whether the scene is represented with sufficient skill to stir a sympathetic response in the uncommitted bystander. But that is a different question from the one that asks whether the emotion fits the occasion—or whether the occasion, however natural, is worth building a poem around. By the late twentieth century it seems clear that Snodgrass, and those who followed him, had established the legitimacy of parent-child relations as a subject for poetry.

Within the span of another generation we began to see many instances of poems attesting to strong feelings about children. If women in recent years have pioneered such poems, men have not been far behind. In an era that has seen the role of men in their children's lives expand well beyond a stern presence at the dinner table, male poets too have found occasion to probe the complexities of parental affection.

Mark Jarman makes a point of representing actual, not idealized children in "Dressing My Daughters," implicitly contrasting them with Longfellow's "Children's Hour" confections:

> But living children, somebody's real daughters,
> They do become more real.
> They say, "Stop it!" and "Give it back!"
> And "I don't want to!"

And David Yezzi builds a lovely poem around his relationship with his young daughter, whom he has discreetly allowed to win at tennis:

> After,
> we sprint
>
> on the road
> home, our run
> hung with gold
> silk spun
>
> by spiders in
> patchy pines.
> The threads glint
> in sidewise lines,
>
> cinches borne
> by the air,
> so loosely worn
> they're hardly there.
>
> —"Let"

These concluding stanzas exemplify what Yvor Winters called the postsymbolist method, in which natural details become imbued with meanings both concrete and abstract, or local and extended, so that the filaments of spiderweb are understood as just what they are and also as analogous to the delicate, scarcely felt ties of trust and competitive affection connecting father and daughter.

A corollary parental feeling about children, which has not been much explored before our time despite its ubiquity, is diffuse worry. As we have seen, poems on the death of children were rare enough, considering the high child mortality rate in past generations, yet oddly the inevitable anxiety that all parents feel about their children rarely made its way into the verse of earlier generations. Stepping outside our own traditions, we find a hint of it in a poem by the ancient Chinese poet Bai Juyi, on his three-year-old daughter, whom he apologizes for thinking about:

> Ashamed—to find that I have not a sage's heart:
> I cannot resist vulgar thoughts and feelings.
> Henceforward I am tied to things outside myself:
> My only reward—the pleasure I am getting now.
> If I am spared the grief of her dying young,
> Then I shall have the trouble of getting her married.
>
> —"Remembering Golden Bells," tr. Arthur Waley

As we know from a subsequent poem, he was not spared that grief, but this poem expresses, in the face of a well-justified worry, a bravado once considered an appropriate masculine emotional armor in east and west alike.

By contrast, in our own tradition and time, Alicia Stallings, in her poem "Whethering," shows herself attuned to the subrational worries that can trouble the sleep of parents of young children.

> The rain is haunted;
> I had forgotten.
> My children are two hours abed
> And yet I rise
> Hearing behind the typing of the rain,

Its abacus and digits,
A voice calling me again . . .

She isn't superstitious; she is at pains to identify, or at least locate, the sources of her anxiety:

It isn't them I hear, it's
Something formless that fidgets
Beyond the window's benighted mirror . . .

The problem is something deep in memory, associated with the weather, ominous and ghostly: "Rain is a kind of recollection," she says, though of what, exactly, we cannot be sure. Nevertheless, our involuntary attentiveness rules us

As though by choices that we didn't make and never wanted,
As though by the dead and misbegotten.

And of course sometimes the dread is justified. In our favored age when infant mortality is a rarity, parents who lose a very young child are not only grief-stricken but stunned by a loss that had previously seemed a remote possibility. How does one honor a flesh-and-blood child one never had a chance to know?

I, who never kissed your head,
Lay these ashes in their bed;
That which I could do have done.
Now farewell, my newborn son.

—Yvor Winters, "A Leave-Taking"

Sometimes the infant who died lives on in the parent's mind, growing older in the imagination's parallel universe as he might have in the actual one, through childhood and teens until, as Dana Gioia suggests in "Majority,"

Now you are twenty-one.
Finally, it makes sense

that you have moved away
into your own afterlife.

Indeed, loss takes many forms. It can also involve the painful and complicated feelings for the child that is not there, the child lost through miscarriage or abortion. An early and classical elegy in this vein is Gwendolyn Brooks's "The Mother," a poem in which the speaker suggests there were multiple abortions in her past but is unstinting in acknowledging both her responsibility and her grief:

Believe that even in my deliberateness I was not deliberate.
Though why should I whine,
Whine that the crime was other than mine?—
Since anyhow you are dead.
Or rather, or instead,
You were never made.
But that too, I am afraid,
Is faulty: oh, what shall I say, how is the truth to be said?
You were born, you had body, you died.
It is just that you never giggled or planned or cried.
Believe me, I loved you all.
Believe me, I knew you, though faintly, and I loved, I loved you
All.

Men as well as women can feel such losses acutely. A. M. Juster captures the difficulty of explaining the loss of a child (through miscarriage or a medically necessary abortion) to his small son:

Although I know my boy does not intend
More pain, he asks about the nameless son
We lost three months before he was conceived.
I have no words to tell him how we grieved.

—"Fugitive Son"

Poems of this sort reveal a problem that is in a way the inverse of sentimentality: rather than generating an emotion that outweighs the situation behind it, they risk deploying words that are inadequate to the magnitude of the feeling that motivates them ("I have no words to tell him"). That they succeed in moving the reader is an indication of both the poet's tact and the reader's experience and sympathy.

The Scottish poet Don Paterson explores a more complex situation in his poem "The Swing." The speaker has purchased a swing set for his two boys and is setting it up in the back yard as his wife looks on. The boys are identified as "the here-and-here-to-stay," and we come to understand that they are thus contrasted with one who is not here to stay. Only his wife knows, the speaker says, why he works so solemnly. He sets up the swing, then steps back to admire what he's done,

> and saw within its frail trapeze
> the child that would not come
> of what we knew had two more days
> before we sent it home[3]

We must infer that the wife is pregnant and that the two of them have chosen to end the pregnancy. Some rather obscure writing ensues in the following stanzas, in which the poet struggles with the implications of their decision, but the final stanza is both clear and moving. The about-to-be-aborted fetus is imagined as a small girl who might have sat (but never actually will) on the seat of that swing:

> I gave the empty seat a push
> and nothing made a sound
> and swung between two skies to brush
> her feet upon the ground

The would-be child, a figment really, only fleetingly makes contact with the world. But it is the pronoun in the final line that, in giving a human actuality to the "nothing" in the second line, wrenches the reader's heart.

Parents writing about children defines one type of familial poem. *Adults writing about their aging parents* defines another. In this genre women poets have often taken the lead. In fact, one possible reason for the surge in poems about parent-child relations may be that the office of poet is now assumed at least as often by women as by men. And in the present generation women have not felt constrained to avoid areas of experience traditionally reserved for women. The resulting poems have sometimes taken surprising directions. Kathleen Jamie uses her poem "Moon" to look back at her mother from her position as a grown woman:

> *Moon,*
> I said, *We're both scarred now.*
>
> *Are they quite beyond you,*
> *the simple words of love? Say them.*
> *You are not my mother;*
> *with my mother, I waited unto death.*

And in "The Photograph" Ellen Bryant Voigt depicts a woman's complex relationship with a mother and a daughter simultaneously:

> Black as a crow's wing was what they said
> about my mother's hair. Even now,
> back home, someone on the street
> will stop me to recall my mother,
> how beautiful she was,
> first among her sisters.
> In the photograph, her hair
> is a spill of ink below the white beret,
> a swell of dark water. And her eyes as dark,
> her chin lifted, that brusque defining posture
> she had just begun in her defense.
> Seventeen, on her own,
> still a shadow in my father's longing—nothing
> the camera could record foretold
> her restlessness, the years of shrill
> unspecified despair, the clear reproach
> of my life, just beginning.
>
> The horseshoe hung in the neck of the tree sinks
> deeper into heartwood every season.

Sometimes I hear the past
hum in my ear, its cruel perfected music,
as I turn from the stove
or stop to braid my daughter's thick black hair.

The poem is told from the point of view of a daughter who is herself the mother of a young child.

The speaker's mother, now apparently dead, is still held up to her as possessed of an exceptional beauty that the speaker evidently believes she cannot match. But the mother's personality, with its "shrill / unspecified despair," its "clear reproach / of my life," evidently left much to be desired. And her reproach[4] has, like a horseshoe sinking into the heartwood of a tree, choked the speaker, who still hears "its cruel perfected music" when she turns to braid the black hair her daughter has inherited. Far from a celebration of filial affection, the poem is an exploration of the complexities of feeling that can pass from mother to daughter to daughter.

A major reason for the proliferation of poems about elderly family members is the extended life span of present generations. For the first time it has become common for people to interact with parents who have lived into their eighties and beyond, who no longer serve as primary authorities or guides, and who may have lost much of their mental acuity. How does one deal emotionally with a parent who was once a wise mentor and is now willful, childlike, confused, and uncertain? Seamus Heaney contrasts himself as a youngster, following his father as he plowed the fields, with his father now:

I was a nuisance, tripping, falling,
Yapping always. But today
It is my father who keeps stumbling
Behind me, and will not go away.

   —"Follower"

Whether the father in the poem is or is not still living hardly affects the force of the statement: what does matter is his persistence as at once a presence, an impediment, and a cynosure, bound to the speaker by shared history and unbreakable affection.

The loss of a still-living father is felt even more poignantly in David Mason's poem "Swimmers on the Shore." Once, as a child, the speaker climbed on his father's shoulders as he stood in waist-deep water, then dived off, secure in the knowledge that he would be protected. But now he sees that his father has become "shrunken":

> I see him cast for words, and fail.
> Though talking never came with ease,
> it is as if my father's memories
> dissolve in a cedar-darkened pool,
> while I no longer am aware
> which of us goes fishing there.

We're forced, with the speaker, to watch the slow unraveling of his father's mind: "I cannot, / from his unfinished sentences, / quite fathom where or who he is." And yet this uncertainty in no way threatens the bond between them. That is what makes the situation unbearable. The ties of affection are still as strong as ever, but there is a devastating realization that something is irretrievably slipping away:

> There is no doubt,
> despite his loss of memory,
> and though the words could not be found,
> it's I who have begun to drown.

Why is that last line so affecting? It seems contrary to fact: the speaker is in full control of his faculties and in the prime of his life. He can act as a lifeline for his enfeebled father. But the "I" that was once dependent, deferential, comfortable in the assurance of his father's solidity and permanence, that earliest and deepest part of the self, must now be—or start to be—abandoned, allowed to sink slowly beneath time's waves. This is an experience most people endure with the death of a parent, but it is excruciatingly and ambiguously protracted with the slow and uneven but inexorable loss of capacity that often accompanies extreme old age. Until now this modern affliction was a generally unexplored topic for poetry.

. . . .

Changes in both social and literary conventions have conspired over the last half-century to bring concerns with family matters, and particularly with the relations between children and parents, into the ambit of poetry. Not only have women in our time become equally represented and respected among serious poets, but men—at least in the social classes from which most poets emerge—have become notably more engaged in the emotional lives of their children and their parents. And both sexes have become more psychologically minded. Partly as a result, the range of subjects open by convention to poets has broadened considerably. The lyric is no longer concerned principally with self-analysis and self-exposition. Able now to examine an expanded range of affections—not just between man and woman but also between two people of the same sex and between parent and child—it does so with less dependence on artifice and convention, if not always with greater insight.

What this brief survey shows, apart from the quite varied styles and techniques employed by the poets of these years, is the progressive complexity of the familial relations depicted, and the nuanced emotions that inevitably accompany them. The relative thinness of earlier poetic tradition in these areas of experience places a burden of perceptiveness and invention on poets that not all can shoulder with grace. Those who are intensely invested in the subject face the difficult task of finding the words that will make the human connection as essential to the reader as it is to them. This is true regardless of the matter at hand, but the task is hardest when the subject is most central to the self. With that in mind, we can understand why many of the poems I've mentioned here represent both a technical and a psychological breakthrough.

NOTES

1. Sabine Durrant, "Sharon Olds: Confessions of a Divorce," London, *The Guardian* (26 January 2013).

2. Mark Poster, *Critical Theory of the Family* (Continuum, 1978).

3. Paterson uses no punctuation in this poem.

4. The syntax of this passage ("the clear reproach / of my life") allows for two possible interpretations: that the speaker's mother reproaches her daughter's life, or that the daughter's life is taken as a reproach to her mother. In either case their relationship is clearly marked by tension.

II. POETIC LINES

6

SHORT OF BREATH
Poems in a Narrow Compass

What is verse, after all, but rhythmic speech? The sentences we construct to express our ideas can usually be made rhythmic by means of a few adjustments. In general, but by no means always, the process involves arranging syllables so that those receiving more stress alternate with those receiving less. And lines are generally contrived to end at either grammatical junctures or rhetorical break-points. It happens that the typical phrase-lengths of much English literary prose match up quite well with tetrameter and pentameter lines of verse, so that little violence need be done to versify it. Here, for example, is the opening of John Banville's sequel to James's *Portrait of a Lady,* called *Mrs. Osmond:* "It had been a day of agitations and alarms, of smoke and steam and grit. Even yet she felt, did Mrs. Osmond, the awful surge and rhythm of the train's wheels, beating on and on within her." It's not hard to turn this into:

> A day of agitations and alarms,
> of smoke and steam and grit; and even yet
> she felt the surge and rhythm of the train
> still beating on and on inside her head.

The point here is not to make an exact duplicate, but to show that the iambic pentameter line readily accommodates the syntactic units of English literary prose. So easily is the transition accomplished, indeed, that even superb metrists may occasionally fall into a kind of discursive blank-verse rambling when the muse of pith and compression momentarily abandons them.

The situation is quite different in the case of very short meters such as dimeters, to which I want to devote my attention here. Poems in these meters can often be arresting, but they do not in general imitate the rhythms of literary prose—or even colloquial speech. Instead they often adopt a tone of urgency, characterized by the short clauses people tend to employ at critical moments. They mark off those clauses by line-endings and often by rhyme, as in Herrick's "Upon a Delaying Lady":

> Come, come away,
> Or let me go;
> Must I here stay
> Because you're slow,
> And will continue so?
> Troth, lady, no.[1]

The penultimate line is in trimeter; all the rest are in dimeter. They amount to an ingenious and convincingly short-tempered way of saying, "Just because you are tardy by nature I don't see why I should have to wait for you."

In a rare song of but two stresses per line, Thomas Campion likewise employs only short phrases whose ends match the line-ends, but does so using an exclusively trochaic meter:

> Follow, follow,
> Though with mischief
> Arm'd, like whirlwind,
> Now she flies thee;
> Time can conquer
> Love's unkindness;
> Love can alter
> Time's disgraces;
> Till death faint not
> Then, but follow.
> Could I catch that
> Nimble traitor,
> Scornful Laura,
> Swift foot Laura,

Soon then would I
Seek avengement.
What's th'avengement?
Even submissely
Prostrate then to
Beg for mercy.

 —"Follow, Follow"

A modern-day Laura might have called this sexual harassment. We do not know what music Campion might have set this poem to; it comes from his theoretical *Observations on the Art of English Poesie,* a treatise rightly called "cranky" by John Hollander.[2] Having previously discussed longer lines, and at last coming to the dimeter, Campion comments: "If any shall demand the reason why this number, being in itself simple, is placed after so many compounded numbers, I answer, because I hold it a number too licentiate for a higher place, and in respect of the rest imperfect; yet is it passing graceful in our English tongue, and will excellently fit the subject of a madrigal, or any other lofty or tragical matter." The word *licentiate,* to Campion, evidently meant "free from rules," or "unrestrained," rather than "licentious." This is curious, because many modern writers would find it anything but unrestrained. Yet as we shall see, there have been productive and ingenious dissents.

In the twentieth century, the brief flare of Imagism encouraged the use of short meters, which suggested fragmentary moments of inspiration outside the domain of reason and logic. The poems of H.D. capture this sensibility most successfully. Here is the first part of "Sea Iris":

Weed, moss-weed,
root tangled in sand,
sea-iris, brittle flower,
one petal like a shell
is broken,
and you print a shadow
like a thin twig.

Fortunate one,
scented and stinging,

> rigid myrrh-bud,
> camphor-flower,
> sweet and salt—you are wind
> in our nostrils.

It cannot be said that such poems adhere to a regular meter, but clearly no lines have more than three stresses, and most have two. H.D.'s characteristic sentence structure is well suited to the short-lined poem: a series of phrasal epithets followed at some point by a simple verb of direct address. The effect is chant-like, as if a priestess were invoking a deity.

It is evident that short meters can be written with considerable metrical variation, so that it often makes more sense to speak of a "two-beat line" than to characterize the poems as iambic dimeter. When T. S. Eliot turns to short lines in "The Waste Land," the passages again show wide deflection from traditional iambics, even though their two-beat pulse, unpunctuated but cued by sporadic rhyme, is easily perceived.

> Elizabeth and Leicester
> Beating oars
> The stern was formed
> A gilded shell
> Red and gold
> The brisk swell
> Rippled both shores
> Southwest wind
> Carried down stream
> The peal of bells
> White towers

Again we encounter broken syntax in which some sentences can be discerned ("The brisk swell rippled both shores." "Southwest wind carried down stream the peal of bells.") while other fragments hover about, lending atmosphere but not grammatical coherence.

It is only a small step down from the ecstatic raptures of H.D. to the visionary insights of Samuel Menashe. With almost no punctuation, a loose rhyme scheme, and a floating, sometimes indeterminate syntax, Menashe creates, in "Eyes," an oracular poem with two stresses in each line:

Eyes have their day
Before the tongue
That slips to say
What they see at once
Without word play,
Betraying no one

Be deaf, dumb, a dunce
With cleft palate
Bereft of speech
Open eyes possess
That wilderness
No tongue can breach[3]

Don't bother speaking, says the poet (using words), since the tongue will distort what the eyes see clearly. The first line in the second stanza has arguably three stresses, but the rhyme at the end marks it off clearly from the following line (which shakes up the iambic rhythm with the trochaic *palate*), after which the poem returns to the regular iambic dimeter pattern (save for an anapest at the start of the antepenultimate line). The poem demonstrates its point by its unstable grammar and uncertain references. (Who is addressed at the start of the second stanza? Does the phrase "Bereft of speech" belong to the one being enjoined there or to the eyes celebrated at the end?) The poet insists that vision is not prone to such ambiguities—though a psychologist or a detective might demur.

A virtuoso of short measures, Menashe is capable of paring his dimeter lines down to three syllables apiece, as he shows in "Anonymous":

Truth to tell,
Seldom told
Under oath,
We live lies

>And grow old
>Self disguised—
>Who are you
>I talk to?

Here again, rhyme, though irregular and not always pure, reinforces the line-end pauses to clarify the stripped-down syntax and enhance the rhetorical force of the final question. Still, the syntax is not unambiguous. One might paraphrase the poem thus: *In truth (though truth is seldom told, even under oath), we live falsely (with false fronts? with false stories?) and grow old disguised from our selves. So baffling are these disguises, I am unsure who you (my interlocutor) are.*

An even shorter poem in the same three-syllable mode, and also using rhyme, is one of Menashe's most gnomic and most powerful:

>Pity us
>by the sea
>on the sands
>so briefly

The extreme ellipsis and compression of the poem compel the reader to elaborate its implications. Its strength derives from the reader's active engagement in realizing the fuller meanings behind the terse expression. A reading with a slight pause after each line will invest each phrase with a weight it would not have as part of a rapidly spoken sentence.

I have used the term "pause" as a convenience, but I do not wish to suggest that each line, when spoken, is to be followed by a noticeable interruption in sound of the sort we imply when we speak of a caesura. There are many degrees of pause, ranging from the emphatic down to the almost indiscernible. Experienced performers of poems or verse plays are capable of suggesting a juncture between two lines by tone of voice—for example, finishing one line on a high pitch, then starting the next on a lower one—while maintaining almost equal spacing between the words. There will always be tension between the rhythm suggested by the lines of a poem and the implied rhythms of idiomatic speech. That tension gives spoken verse its distinctive quality and tests the expertise of the person reciting it. For our purposes it is enough to recognize that even in unrhymed poems rife with enjambments one must assume the writers intended the line-endings to be rhetorically meaningful, whether because they coincide with syntactic junctures or because they counterpoint them. Performers are obliged to employ various strategies to meet the resulting challenge.

So far we have seen rhyme used to cue the line-endings and thus help the listener parse the poem's syntax. But as Menashe demonstrates in an untitled poem, brief hesitations quite unaided by rhyme can also work effectively to lay out the syntax of a perfectly idiomatic seventeen-word statement:

> These stone steps
> beveled by feet
> endear the dead
> to me as I climb
> them every night

Here we have two stresses per line, with implied pauses of varying degrees between lines, like feet ascending steps, and the reader quickly perceives the poem's rhythm. No cues of rhyme or punctuation are needed. Every line except the fourth has three words; the fourth, with five, replaces the second iamb with an anapest. The poem functions, in other words, just as blank verse does in the five-stress environment, although the words must be more carefully chosen. Multisyllabic words and complex subordinate clauses would be much harder to accommodate.

Not all twentieth-century poems in short meters come out of the Imagist tradition. For a contrasting example of rhymed dimeter with a much more august and rational bearing in the moralizing plain-style tradition of Walter Raleigh,[4] take "To the Reader," an acid commentary on scholarship by J. V. Cunningham:

> Time will assuage,
> Time's verses bury
> Margin and page
> In commentary,
>
> For gloss demands
> A gloss annexed

> Till busy hands
> Blot out the text,
>
> And all's coherent.
> Search in this gloss
> No text inherent:
> The text was loss.
>
> The gain is gloss.

We are dealing here with a complex idea, but the meter forces compression, and the compression challenges the reader: What is assuaged by time? What are time's verses? How does gloss blot out text, and what does it mean to say the text was loss? These questions surely have answers, but readers must dig into their own experience to discern them and in the process realize the poem. An ironist might say each reader is forced to provide his own gloss.

Even at this half-way point in our survey we can see that short meters do not constrain a poem's subject matter. They do, however, affect tone, and they often impose on the reader the obligation to elaborate the implications of a tightly compressed (and therefore elliptical) expression. At the same time, by forcing the poet to express ideas in short clauses and to slow down the rate at which those clauses accost the reader, they create a field in which syllables must be chosen with extreme care and each must justify the prominence given it by the poem's pacing.

Belle Turnbull, another poet partial to short meters and the visionary mode of H.D. and Menashe, hews more closely than either of them do to normal grammar in "Brother Juniper":

> Under the primrose cliffs
> Lives an old juniper,
> Claws like a hippogriff's
> Fastened round a rock.
> Warworn his trunk is,
> Rigid his fiber,
> Ribboned his bark.
>   For all his payment,
> Wrung as a tear is,

Pale on his raiment
Of ashen green:
Four frosty berries,
Issue of the ages,
Juiceless and lean.

The first four lines can be read as trimeter (though the second is ambiguous), but thereafter the lines are clearly dimeter. And while the syntax is straightforward, it is also much simplified, consisting of a series of epithets applied to the juniper. After the first four lines the only verb is "is"; the remaining lines are thus freed to serve as serial descriptive elements.

Even more radical is Turnbull's "High Trail," unpunctuated in the manner of Menashe and consisting mostly of one- or two-word lines, each with two stresses, and with a syntax sufficiently indeterminate that the poem can be read line by line from top to bottom or from bottom to top:

The   trail   is
thin   dear
loneliest
the one road
vein-strait
the one road
wheel-clear
foot-wise
celibate
thin   dear
the   trail   is

The extra spaces in the first two and last two lines are evidently deliberate and intended as instructions to the reader to slow these lines down in pronouncing them. The stream of words emulates its subject: this is a trail that must be carefully walked and can be traversed in either direction.

By contrast, Elizabeth Bishop positions "The Moose" in a much more matter-of-fact world, constructing it as a series of complex discursive sentences (the first one is six stanzas long), built on a largely two-beat measure, with rhyme marking her line-endings and frequent assonance and alliteration throughout:

the sweet peas cling
to their wet white string
on the whitewashed fences;
bumblebees creep
inside the foxgloves,
and evening commences.

From time to time the measure expands to admit three beats, but then returns to two:

One stop at Bass River.
Then the Economies
Lower, Middle, Upper;
Five Islands, Five Houses,
where a woman shakes a tablecloth
out after supper.

As the poem demonstrates, it is possible to write an extended work in a short measure and keep the reader engaged throughout. ("The Moose" consists of twenty-eight six-line stanzas.) The poem is also notable for its everyday language. It resorts to virtually none of the elliptical syntax or oracular pronouncements we saw in Eliot, Menashe, Cunningham, and Turnbull. The final stanza maintains that tone of voice while expanding its syntactic range:

by craning backward,
the moose can be seen
on the moonlit macadam;
then there's a dim
smell of moose, an acrid
smell of gasoline.

In contrast to the other lines (and the majority of lines in the poem), the fourth and fifth lines of this stanza break up larger clauses at unusual points (between an adjective and its noun); but the half-rhymes link them to other lines of the poem (*macadam/dim, backward/acrid*). The poem achieves closure with a final full rhyme on *seen/gasoline*.

Contemporary writers, often less beholden to metric niceties, still gravitate to the two-beat line (with allowances for three-beat rhetorical exceptions), still place signposts of rhyme at key junctures, and may allow additional words into the line, departing further from iambics but gaining syntactic solidity, as in Kevin Young's "Hurricane Song" (a variation on "Baby It's Cold Outside") in which I have marked the stresses I would use:

Lády, won't you wáit
óut the húrricane

all níght at mý place—
wé'll take cóver like

the lámps & Í'll
lét you óil

my scálp. Pléase, I néeds
a góod wóman's hánds

cáught in my háir, túrning
my knóts to bútter.

All níght we'll chúrn.
Dáwn

will léan in too sóon—
you'll léave out ínto

the wét world, wínded
& alóne, knówing

the mé ónly
mídnight sées.

Note the *turning/churn* rhyme, the half-rhymes of *I'll* and *oil*, *into* and *winded*, the sequence of terminal *n*'s in *churn/dawn/lean/soon*, the alliterated *w*'s in *wet world winded*, and the assonance of *alone/knowing/only*. All these devices help to stabilize and structure a poem that the casual reader might initially take, because of its irregular distribution of stresses, to be in free verse.[5]

We have reached a point in the long debates between poets committed to formal structure and those deeply suspicious of it where we might usefully imagine a continuum. At one end are those who seek to fit all expression into a metric scheme, often one with a fixed rhyme pattern, and who believe that even the most recalcitrant ideas can with sufficient ingenuity be molded into the requisite shapes, thereby enhancing the associated emotions. At the other end are those who believe ideas and emotions lose their immediacy and force in being subjected to fixed forms; they renounce allegiance to meter though they still acknowledge that lineation plays a strong role in a poem's effectiveness. Between those poles are various compromises, with meter becoming progressively less important as one moves along the scale from one side to the other.

Even poets who have abandoned metrical verse entirely still now and then find in short lines a useful discipline. A. R. Ammons famously wrote *Tape for the Turn of the Year* on adding machine tape, thus enforcing short lines even though no meter compelled them. Yet his extensive prologue indicates that he sees short lines as a guide to aesthetic rigor, calling for

> clarity & simplicity!
> no muffled talk, fragments
> of phrases, linked
> without logical links,
> strung
> together in obscurities
> supposed to reflect
> density: it's
> a wall
> to obscure emptiness, the
> talk of a posing man who
> must talk
> but who has nothing to
> say: let this song
>   make
> complex things salient
> saliences clear, so
>   there can be some
>   understanding:

If the poem is read aloud with pauses at the line-ends, it sounds awkward and hesitant. Read silently, it moves along quickly enough, its ideas, as Ammons intended, seeming more translucent than they might if couched in dense paragraphs. But it's a stretch to call it a song.

Near the same end of the spectrum is Robert Creeley, whose most famous poem, "I Know a Man," is also in short lines whose stresses do not fall into discernible patterns:

> As I sd to my
> friend, because I am
> always talking,—John, I
>
> sd, which was not his
> name, the darkness sur-
> rounds us, what
>
> can we do against
> it, or else, shall we &
> why not, buy a goddamn big car,
>
> drive, he sd, for
> christ's sake, look
> out where yr going.

Commenting on this poem, Lynn Keller remarks on its departure from standard speech patterns: "Most of the line breaks in 'I Know a Man,' coming midphrase, create hesitations one would not find in relaxed conversation." She adds, "Because of the asyntactic line breaks, the first syllable of each line receives extra emphasis." This, I think, is incorrect. Such line breaks do not automatically confer emphasis. The second line of the third stanza, for example, does not begin with an emphasized syllable. Rather, Creeley has placed his line breaks so that most of them occur before a stressed syllable, and if we are counting stresses, we will note that most (but not all) lines contain two. The third line of the third stanza is an exception, of course. Because there is in fact so little relation between the poem's syntax and its line-endings, one can question whether the lineation serves any purpose for the ear.[6] For the eye its primary function may well be simply to announce that this short piece of writing is in fact a poem.

Regarding the poem's central dilemma—"what can we do / against [the darkness]"—Keller comments, "When the speaker hits upon a possible solution, the poem's rhythms reflect his momentary confidence and sense of liberation; 'buy a goddamn big car' is the poem's only phrase of any length that flows unimpeded."[7] This may be a bit circular—imputing meaning to the form of the line that happens to have that meaning—but it is certainly true that the line by its length, and the time it takes to say it, stands out from the rest of the poem.

What is undeniable is that the lineation of the poem cuts across the clauses at every point but one (the line ending "buy a goddamn big car"), forcing anyone reading it aloud either to ignore the line breaks or to introduce awkward hesitations at irregular intervals. This may have been a deliberate strategy on Creeley's part, and it raises an interesting question: can a poet create a rhythm that violates a poem's syntax while also enhancing its effect? Or to give it a more positive spin, is it possible to establish polyrhythms in which syntax is played off against lineation?

The answer is yes, and the *locus classicus* is not here but in Gwendolyn Brooks's poem "The Pool Players":

We real cool. We
Left school. We

Lurk late. We
Strike straight. We

Sing sin. We
Thin gin. We

Jazz June. We
Die soon.

The syntactic structure is very simple: Eight three-word sentences, each word a single syllable, each sentence beginning with "We." The last words in each pair of sentences rhyme. Alliteration characterizes four of the sentences. Brooks's innovation is to displace the initial "We" of each sentence after the first back to the end of the previous line. This means the first line has four words (and syllables), and the last has two. The result is a syncopated rhythm, forcing a pause after the subject of each sentence and drawing out a moment of expectancy before the verb that follows.[8]

It is vain, I believe, to analyze this poem in terms of traditional iambic patterns. What we have here is a series of lines each with a heavy stress at the end and a spondee of somewhat lesser stress at the start. None of the syllables are unstressed. If the poem were arranged with one complete sentence on each line, the words would receive virtually equal stress and the poem would be much less interesting. It gains a decisive meter and rhetorical force by the stress and the pause resulting from the displacement—and of course by its final isolated, stark two words.

A different kind of displacement is at work in the poems of Kay Ryan—poems with very short lines in which we often find rhyme embedded in unexpected places. It might surprise some readers to encounter, poring through Ryan's work, an orthodox iambic tetrameter poem with a traditional rhyme scheme:

> However carved up or pared down we get,
> we keep on making the best of it
> as though it doesn't matter that
> our acre's down to a square foot.
>
> As though our garden could be one bean
> and we'd rejoice if it flourishes,
> as though one bean could nourish us.

The rhymes are not quite exact, but they are close enough to be unmistakable. I have little doubt that this is the way Ryan conceived the poem originally, but though she published it word for word, she did so only after rearranging it to give it the short lines that we associate with her work:

> However carved up
> or pared down we get,
> we keep on making
> the best of it as though
> it doesn't matter that
> our acre's down to

> a square foot. As
> though our garden
> could be one bean
> and we'd rejoice if
> it flourishes, as
> though one bean
> could nourish us.

> —"The Best of It"

Note that the breaks Ryan introduces in this new pattern are often not the expected ones. The fourth line acquires an extra foot and thereby submerges its rhyme (*get/it*) and in the process throws off the pattern of breaks so that the next rhyme (*that/foot*) is also lost. Instead of a straightforward rhymed tetrameter poem, we have now a poem in two- and three-stress lines, not all of which can be comfortably scanned as iambic. It seems to be unrhymed, yet ghostly echoes can be heard now and then; *bean* is thrown into prominence as a self-rhyme, and the match between *flourish* and *nourish,* though the words occupy different positions, is unmistakable. The poem thus becomes a construction of irregular short lines that break at odd points and harbor submerged rhymes, through which an attentive reader can hear the faint strains of the original rhymed tetrameter poem.

Poems like this, along with the Brooks and Young poems discussed earlier, indicate something important about the perceptual aptitude of readers—something many poets, and most prosodists, do not make sufficient allowance for: readers are capable of hearing more than one rhythmic or metric scheme at a time. One can hear a four-beat rhythm behind a two-beat rhythm. One can hear a predominantly two-beat rhythm, as in the poems by Bishop and Young, even when it is temporarily superseded by a series of three-beat lines. One can readily hear rhythms, like those in the Brooks poem, that the standard nomenclature of iambs and anapests (adapted after all from classical measures of quantity) is ill-suited to describe.

And of course the word *hear* is too narrow to account for the totality of our response. For the perception of rhythmic verse is a matter of a thoroughgoing visceral embrace of certain sound patterns. I. A. Richards stated the matter well in an essay on rhythm and meter:

Metre adds to all the variously fated expectancies which make up rhythm a definite temporal pattern and its effect is not due to our perceiving a pattern in something outside us, but to our becoming patterned ourselves. With every beat of the metre a tide of anticipation in us turns and swings, setting up as it does so extraordinarily extensive sympathetic reverberations. We shall never understand metre so long as we ask, "Why does temporal pattern so excite us?" and fail to realise that the pattern itself is a vast cyclic agitation spreading all over the body, a tide of excitement pouring through the channels of the mind.[9]

I would add that the timing of sometimes minute pauses, their accelerated frequency in short meters, mimics the breathlessness we associate with excitement and haste and so conveys to us an added sense of urgency—not necessarily peril, but an awareness that the matter at hand has a direct and immediate claim on our attention. Poets who use such meters thus put themselves under an implicit obligation to justify that claim.

NOTES

1. Despite initial appearances, I will not proceed chronologically in this essay. I do not wish to suggest that there is a historical progression in the techniques discussed here.

2. Introduction to *Selected Songs of Thomas Campion* (Godine, 1973).

3. All quotations of Menashe's poems are from *Samuel Menashe: New and Selected Poems,* ed. Christopher Ricks (New York: Library of America, 2005). Punctuation and other minor details in this edition differ occasionally from corresponding details as originally published in the poet's own books.

4. For an example, see Raleigh's "Nymph's Reply":

> Thy gowns, thy shoes, thy beds of roses,
> Thy cap, thy kirtle, and thy posies
> Soon break, soon wither, soon forgotten,
> In folly ripe, in reason rotten.

5. To those who object to my use of "free verse" to mean "nonmetrical, nonrhyming lines that closely follow the natural rhythms of speech" (Poetry Foundation): I am aware of the controversies but have long ago given up the search for a less negative, more rigorous, and still defensible definition of the term.

6. At least two of the readings on YouTube do place pauses at line-ends; the effect is like that produced by someone with a slight speech impediment.

7. Lynn Keller, *Re-making It New: Contemporary American Poetry and the Modernist Tradition* (Cambridge University Press, 1987).

8. In every recording I have heard of Brooks reading this poem she places a heavy pause after each "We" at the end of a line. Listeners may debate whether those pauses contribute to meaning or are simply musical.

9. I. A. Richards, "Rhythm and Metre," from *Principles of Literary Criticism*, reprinted in *The Structure of Verse: Modern Essays on Prosody*, ed. Harvey Gross (Fawcett, 1966).

7

THE PHOENIX LINE
History of a Style

It is dangerous to make too much of an association between a metrical pattern and the substance of the matter it conveys. For a proper balance of caution and impudence I will invoke a remark by Simon Jarvis: "The devices of verse have no fixed effects, but readers are seduced into conjecturing effects with them, as they notice poets sinking the most powerful thoughts and feelings into even the most abject little phonetic and printed bits and pieces."[1] I wish to look at several examples, spanning four centuries, of something perhaps a little more than abject—the headless iambic tetrameter line, sometimes called a truncated or catalectic trochaic line, that is, a trochaic tetrameter lacking a final unstressed syllable. It is a line of seven syllables starting and ending with a stress and alternating between stressed and unstressed syllables:

For illustration, take a line from Yeats:

Irish poets, learn your trade.

What makes the meter worth studying is that whole poems have been written in it, though infrequently, over the entire stretch of literature in modern English, and that, as I hope to show here, the poems in this meter have more character, if not thematic content, in common than mere chance would account for. In short, it is a metrical style that often, though not always, brings with it a characteristic set of emotions, a characteristic tonality.

Our earliest example comes from Fulke Greville. Like his good friend Philip Sidney, Greville was a tireless metrical experimenter. We do not know what led him to the catalectic tetrameter line, which pervades the fifty-sixth poem in his *Caelica* collection, better known by its first line: "All my senses, like beacon's flame." Thom Gunn characterizes this rhythm (not shared by the first line) as "a difficult metre that tends to stiffness because of the rather heavy emphasis given to the first syllable," but, as he also notes, "it is used here with great flexibility."[2] Part of that flexibility results from the poet's willingness to vary the meter with lines having an unstressed first syllable:

Up I start believing well
To see if Cynthia were awake;
Wonders I saw, who can tell?
And thus unto myself I spake:

The second and fourth lines here are complete iambic tetrameters and mitigate the poem's tendency to become a chant.

As he nears the end of his discourse Greville takes full advantage of his meter's suitability for pronouncements:

He that lets his Cynthia lie,
Naked on a bed of play
To say prayers ere she die
Teacheth time to run away.
Let no love-desiring heart
In the stars go seek his fate,
Love is only nature's art,
Wonder hinders love and hate.

Note the disyllabic "prayers" in the third line and the imperative mood at the start of the last quatrain quoted. We shall see that mood recur often as we trace the applications of this meter.

We do not know whether he picked it up from Greville, but we do know that Shakespeare made use of the meter in his late plays. Probably the most famous instance is in *The Tempest,* in Ariel's song:

Full fathom five thy father lies;
Of his bones are coral made;
Those are pearls that were his eyes:
Nothing of him that doth fade,
But doth suffer a sea-change
Into something rich and strange.

Sea-nymphs hourly ring his knell.
Hark! now I hear them—Ding-dong, bell.

The first line, of course, is standard iambic tetrameter, fuzzed with alliteration. The remaining lines all start with a stressed syllable, and all except the last
one are seven syllables in length. The last line has eight: it's a standard iambic
tetrameter line with a trochaic first foot—but the second and third syllables,
unstressed, have elided vowels that almost fuse together, making the line all
but indistinguishable metrically from the preceding ones.

Shakespeare's longest and most decisive use of this distinctive line occurs
in "The Phoenix and the Turtle," a poem that begins in the imperative mood, a
grammatical gesture in which phrases often take a trochaic pattern in English
and often lack a final unstressed syllable. ("Pass the salt." "Follow me." "Stay
between the lines." "Don't believe a word he says." "Call me Ishmael."):

Let the bird of loudest lay,
On the sole Arabian tree,
Herald sad and trumpet be,
To whose sound chaste wings obey.

Both the grammatical mood and the four-stress, seven-syllable verse line are
sustained throughout the five introductory stanzas, in which the community
of birds celebrating the two protagonists is called together.

Even when the imperative mood is abandoned for the descriptive indic-
ative, the meter is maintained with remarkable rigor. The only exceptions
occur in the eighth stanza, where unstressed final syllables are admitted in the
two outer lines; the eleventh, where all four lines are complete (acatalectic)
trochaic tetrameters; and the last line of the thirteenth stanza, which is in

iambic tetrameter but so imbued with the tonality of the preceding lines that the deviation is scarcely noticed.

For the Threnos, Shakespeare shifts to a three-line stanza in which all three end-words rhyme. The catalectic trochaic pattern is sternly maintained. The penultimate tercet makes a lapidary pronouncement of fact:

> Truth may seem, but cannot be:
> Beauty brag, but 'tis not she;
> Truth and beauty buried be.

And the final tercet reverts to the imperative mood to solemnize the obsequy.

> To this urn let those repair
> That are either true or fair;
> For these dead birds sigh a prayer.

Note that the last line, consisting entirely of monosyllables, hews to the prevailing pattern by what we might call the force of habit. In normal speech "these" would receive more stress than "For" and "birds" than "dead"—

> For **these** dead **birds** we'll **sigh** a **prayer**

—but of course Shakespeare did not write the line that way, and so strong is the trochaic rhythm in our minds that we say, in conformity with the preceding lines,

> **For** these **dead** birds **sigh** a **prayer**.[3]

A meter this distinctive demands a distinctive name. Rather than the awkward "catalectic trochaic (or headless iambic) tetrameter" I propose to call it the phoenix line, both because it is used so scrupulously throughout "The Phoenix and the Turtle" and because it rises suddenly, after long dormant stretches, in the history of poetry in English.

. . . .

That Ben Jonson was well versed in such measures we need have no doubt, both from his reference (in *The Staple of News,* IV.i) to "My egg-chin'd laureate"

With dimeters, and trimeters, tetrameters,
Pentameters, hexameters, catalectics,
His hyper and his brachy-catalectics,
His pyrrhics, epitrites, and choriambics . . .

and from his graceful use of the line in his "Hymn to Diana":

Queen and huntress, chaste and fair,
Now the sun is laid to sleep,
Seated in thy silver chair,
State in wonted manner keep:
    Hesperus entreats thy light,
    Goddess excellently bright.

Here too we see the imperative used, but now in the context of a paean suitable for a monarch.[4]

• • • •

Two hundred years after Shakespeare and Jonson, following a long period in which poets worked to perfect the heroic couplet, William Blake adapts the phoenix line to a very different sort of poem, marginally less opaque than "The Phoenix and the Turtle" but equally monumental. Set not in the imperative mood but entirely in the interrogative, "The Tyger" is a tour-de-force that avoids statements altogether, consisting instead of nothing but rhetorical questions.

Tyger! Tyger! burning bright
In the forests of the night,
What immortal hand or eye
Could frame thy fearful symmetry?

In what distant deeps or skies
Burnt the fire of thine eyes?
On what wings dare he aspire?
What the hand dare seize the fire?

(Note that "fire" needs two syllables in line six above, but only one in line eight.)

Like Shakespeare in the songs, Blake relaxes the trochaic rhythm at points—for example in the fourth line of the first stanza, which is straight iambic tetrameter. This is obviously deliberate. He might have written:

What immortal hand or eye
Framed thy fearful symmetry?

—but he presumably wanted the auxiliary "Could," which would be answered by "Dare" in the repetition of the stanza at the end of the poem.

Unlike commands in English, questions do not so easily fit the trochaic pattern. The typical question starting with an interrogative word like "what" throws the stress onto the following noun, as in "What child is this?" So Blake starts some of his lines with a conjunction capable of bearing the stress; alternatively, as in the second and third lines below, he simply admits an iambic tetrameter line; or, as in the lines that follow, he interposes an unstressed adjective or article so that the words on either side of it exhibit relatively more stress.

And what shoulder, & what art.
Could twist the sinews of thy heart?
And when thy heart began to beat,
What dread hand? & what dread feet?

What the hammer? what the chain?
In what furnace was thy brain?
What the anvil? what dread grasp
Dare its deadly terrors clasp?

The elliptical questions shortened to fit the meter (in lieu of "What was the hammer? what was the chain?") contribute to the oracular quality of the poem overall and give it an air of mystery—all the stronger because no attempt is made to answer them. In short, the line's tendency to become a chant is exactly what we infer Blake is after in these verses.

. . . .

Blake is often considered a proto-Romantic, but the true Romantic poets were more directly concerned with the liberation of the spirit from perceived social or intellectual straits. When Keats tries his hand at the phoenix line, in "Fancy," he writes a paean to the imagination; but he too chooses the imperative mood, at least for his opening line:

> *Ever let the Fancy roam,*
> Pleasure never is at home:
> At a touch sweet Pleasure melteth,
> Like to bubbles when rain pelteth;
> *Then let winged Fancy wander*
> Through the thought still spread beyond her:
> *Open wide the mind's cage-door,*
> She'll dart forth, and cloudward soar.
> *O sweet Fancy! let her loose;*
> Summer's joys are spoilt by use,
> And the enjoying of the Spring
> Fades as does its blossoming;

And even though the poem proceeds through a description of cozy rustic comforts while the poet urges the freeing of the imagination, the imperative mood recurs frequently in the lines I have italicized. The tone of the poem, however, is notably different. Gone is the oracular manner, which is not congenial to Keats; present instead is the description—not seen so far in this meter, of abundant natural detail. As we see in the passage quoted above, unstressed final syllables add a trochaic leavening to the meter, even while other lines make the categorical pronouncements ("Summer's joys are spoilt by use") that we've come to associate with this style of writing. The thrust of the poem is summed up in the final couplet, which recapitulates the opening lines:

> Let the wingèd Fancy roam,
> Pleasure never is at home.

In tone "Fancy" represents a considerable departure from the poems we've looked at so far, in that it is less oracular, less incantatory, more inclined to celebrate the pleasures of home and hearth even while paradoxically extolling the unfettered imagination. To a large extent this quality reflects Keats's own predilections and his times,[5] but in spite of these tonal differences the frequent resort to the imperative mood and the gnomic utterance, both illustrated in the summary couplet just quoted, link the poem to the others we have been surveying.

. . . .

W. B. Yeats, reviving in old age the phoenix that had burned with the youthful Keats, gives us "Under Ben Bulben"—a poem that, like many of its predecessors, begins in the imperative mood:

> Swear by what the sages spoke
> Round the Mareotic Lake
> That the Witch of Atlas knew,
> Spoke and set the cocks a-crow.

It is interesting that Yeats adopts this meter for his final testament as poet and Irish patriot. It has something of the monumental quality he evidently thought appropriate to the occasion, and he uses it to issue proclamations that take full advantage of the meter's decisive tone.

The poem, in six parts, does not hew strictly to the meter set out in the four lines quoted above. Aphoristic in tone, stating what Yeats took to be general truths, it disparages the fear of death, maintains that violence clarifies the mind, and urges the importance of artistic creation. In doing so it offers an eccentric synopsis of western art since the Renaissance and enjoins Irish poets, in particular, to celebrate their history and their people in well-crafted verse.

The verse makes no attempt at metrical orthodoxy: unstressed first syllables occur frequently, though not so often as to destroy the overall trochaic drone. But by the sixth section Yeats has so far departed from the metrical template that only two lines, the first and fifth, conform to the seven-syllable trochaic pattern, while the rest are in regular iambics, except for an anapestic fourth foot in line six:

> Under bare Ben Bulben's head
> In Drumcliff churchyard Yeats is laid.
> An ancestor was rector there
> Long years ago, a church stands near,
> By the road an ancient cross.

No marble, no conventional phrase;
On limestone quarried near the spot
By his command these words are cut:
  Cast a cold eye
  On life, on death.
  Horseman, pass by!

The concluding epitaph is, of course, in iambic dimeter with standard trochaic substitutions.

. . . .

We might expect the phoenix line, uncommon even in the days when "metrical poetry" was a redundancy, to have dropped from sight upon Yeats's death, but the outnumbered twentieth-century conservators of the metrical tradition decreed otherwise.[6] W. H. Auden makes effective use of the line in "Lullaby":

Lay your sleeping head, my love,
Human on my faithless arm;
Time and fevers burn away
Individual beauty from
Thoughtful children, and the grave
Proves the child ephemeral:
But in my arms till break of day
Let the living creature lie,
Mortal, guilty, but to me
The entirely beautiful.

Unsurprisingly, the poem begins in the imperative mood and proceeds, in lines three through six, to the statement of general truths or *sententiae*. The final four lines of the stanza are once again in the imperative mood but imbued for all that with a feeling of deep affection. Only one line in the stanza, the iambic seventh, violates the metrical template.

The final stanza, entirely in the prevailing meter, begins almost as if it were an extension of "The Phoenix and the Turtle": "Beauty, midnight, vision dies." But once again it descends from the universal to the immediate human situation, while reverting to the imperative mood: "Let the winds . . . show";

"Find the mortal world enough." Two final injunctions, also having the force of imperatives, close the poem: "Noons of dryness find you fed"; "Nights of insult let you pass." The poem, which flirts with but does not succumb to sentimentality, is probably more successful than any since Greville's work at marrying universal observations with depictions of human desire.[7]

Philip Larkin also makes successful use of the meter in his two-stanza poem "First Sight," a description, at once delicate and ominous, of newborn lambs' first encounter with the world on a winter morning:

> As they wait beside the ewe,
> Her fleeces wetly caked, there lies
> Hidden round them, waiting too,
> Earth's immeasurable surprise.
> They could not grasp it if they knew,
> What so soon will wake and grow
> Utterly unlike the snow.

The second and fifth lines in this (second) stanza soften the meter by placing iambs in the first position. The effect is to emphasize, by contrast, the starkness of the last two lines

. . . .

My final and most recent example of the phoenix line in successful use comes from America. Gwendolyn Brooks in her mock epic *The Anniad* employs the line throughout, infusing it with a slightly satirical tone nicely captured in her first stanza, which in describing her heroine begins to no one's surprise in the imperative mood:

> Think of sweet and chocolate,
> Left to folly or to fate,
> Whom the higher gods forgot,
> Whom the lower gods berate;
> Physical and underfed
> Fancying on the featherbed
> What was never and is not.

The poem follows Brooks's heroine, the eponymous Annie, a rather naïve young woman, from her youthful longing for a dashing and decisive man, through her encounters with a flawed avatar who is plucked up and sent off to war, to her attempts to rebuild a life with him on his return, and on to her final disillusion. Brooks sets herself the difficult task of adhering closely to the phoenix line (she only occasionally admits an unstressed syllable at the line's start or finish) while narrating significant events (thus departing much of the time from the imperative mood or the aphoristic statement) and at the same time maintaining a satirical tone that is at once amused, ironic, and sympathetic.

Although the mode of epic—even mock epic—is narrative, the phoenix line is better suited to summary than to the detailing of progressive action. So the movement in this poem proceeds mainly by recapitulating the various stages attained by the protagonists. Thus, near the end of the poem, as the denouement approaches, we have this stanza:

> But the culprit magics fade.
> Stoical the retrograde.
> And no music plays at all
> In the inner, hasty hall
> Which compulsion cut from shade.—
> Frees her lover. Drops her hands.
> Shorn and taciturn she stands.

Note how in the sixth line of this stanza the meter requires the poet to drop subject pronouns from her sentences. The effect is a bit like that of the caption frame in a silent film.

The actions of Annie's lover at this stage are narrated through imperatives:

> —Close your fables and fatigues;

> Kill that fanged flamingo foam
> And the fictive gold that mocks;
> Shut your rhetorics in a box;
> Pack compunction and go home.

The last two stanzas of the poem are introduced by the formula—in the imperative mood—that opened it: "Think of tweaked and twenty-four" and "Think of almost thoroughly / Derelict and dim and done." The poem ends with its heroine "Kissing in her kitchenette / The minuets of memory." Only the final line receives a softening unstressed first syllable.

．　．　．　．

Odd though it is, neither quite trochaic nor quite iambic, the phoenix line is remarkably persistent through the long course of English verse. Yet most poets would agree it is not for all markets. While, as we have seen, it can be employed in a diverse range of contexts—from song to narrative to philosophical musing to satire—it brings with it affinities with certain inherent stress patterns of English speech, specifically a preference for the imperative mood and the emphatic statement of general maxims. It blends with other lines— both iambic and trochaic—and thus allows poets with a strong command of their craft to modulate the tone and extend the emotional range of the works in which it appears.

Fundamentally, however, it seems best suited to commands and to contexts in which a persistent, infectious rhythm is important. The meter can capture the magical, the mythical, and the mysterious, as Shakespeare, Jonson, and Blake demonstrate. Fancy may roam in its precincts, as Keats would have it. It can issue proclamations (with Yeats) or caption significant moments (with Brooks). In combination with more usual iambic meters it can have a soothing and restorative effect, as Auden demonstrates. But offered straight, without the softening effect of unstressed syllables before or after, it is capable of dispelling illusions when summoned by realists like Fulke Greville, who employed it when he counseled:

None can well behold with eyes
But what underneath him lies.

NOTES

1. "For a Poetics of Verse," *PMLA*, 125: 4 (2010), 931.
2. Introduction to *Selected Poems of Fulke Greville* (University of Chicago Press, 2009), p. 26.
3. See Nicholas Myklebust's discussion of prototypes and priming in "Rhythmic Cognition in

Late Medieval Lyrics," in D. Wehrs and T. Blake, eds., *The Palgrave Handbook of Affect Studies and Textual Criticism* (Macmillan, 2017), 577–608.

4. Robert Herrick, of the Tribe of Ben, wrote his mentor a suitable epitaph in the same measure:

> Here lies Jonson, with the rest
> Of the poets; but the Best.
> Reader, wouldst thou more have known?
> Ask his Story, not this Stone.
> That will speak what this can't tell
> Of his glory. *So farewell.*

Herrick used the measure dexterously in several other short poems, among them "Cherry-Ripe" and "His Request to Julia."

5. Thomas Moore's translations of Anacreon, published in 1800, were no doubt familiar to Keats. Moore's "anacreontics" did not consistently hew to the meter of the phoenix line, but one can imagine Keats taking both mood and meter from such passages as this, from Ode V:

> Buds of roses, virgin flowers,
> Cull'd from Cupid's balmy bowers,
> In the bowl of Bacchus steep,
> Till with crimson drops they weep!
> Twine the rose, the garland twine,
> Every leaf distilling wine;
> Drink and smile, and learn to think
> That we were born to smile and drink.

6. Well before Yeats's death, in fact, Robert Frost had published "To the Thawing Wind," most of whose lines are phoenix lines, virtually all of which are cast in the imperative mood. A sampling:

> Give the buried flower a dream;
> Make the settled snowbank steam;
> Find the brown beneath the white;
> But whate'er you do tonight,
> Bathe my window, make it flow,
> Melt it as the ice will go;
> Melt the glass and leave the sticks
> Like a hermit's crucifix . . .

7. I note parenthetically that Auden's title, "Lullaby," is also Shakespeare's refrain in the fairies' song from *A Midsummer Night's Dream* (II.ii), a song likewise cast in this meter and largely in the imperative mood. The refrain goes "Lulla, lulla, lullaby, lulla, lulla, lullaby."

8

ON THE TRANSLATION OF POETRY

A glance through the pages of any large-circulation magazine featuring poetry will show how rare are the instances of metered verse, especially verse making use of rhyme, in the poems currently being published. Most poets, but not all, have come to feel that such formal elements are too constraining and are a bit outmoded besides. Writing in a discernible form, it is widely believed, shows the poet to be out of step and out of touch. (Besides, it's hard to do it well.) As a result, many readers have come to expect that a poem of our time will be essentially lineated prose, but of an imaginative or fantastical sort, maybe grammatical, maybe not, with loosened or non-existent logical connections, an unconventional air of enigma or mystery, and a notable emotional and linguistic intensity. Writers will not offer, and readers will not expect, a perceptible pulse and a matching of sounds whose musical qualities might seize and embed themselves in the receptive ear and mind.

In such an environment a translator wishing to produce a new English version of earlier metrical (and often rhymed) poetry in another language is at something of a loss. For the originating poet (a Baudelaire, say, or a Rilke) took it for granted that the musical elements of rhyme and meter were essential components of the verses he wrote; the poems depended on these aspects of their form for their effect, and readers would need to feel the sway of meter and the punctuation of rhyme, ranging from subtle to emphatic, to experience the entire effect of the poems. So, to properly represent such French or German (or Spanish, Norwegian, or Russian) poems, the translator would have to create, to the best of his or her abilities, a metrical and rhymed English equivalent, even though (a) it is nearly impossible to produce such an equivalent while staying true to the exact meaning and nuance of the original, and (b) most readers, it is claimed, do not expect poems to sound like that, cannot hear the difference meter makes, and do not much care in any case. Why then undertake such a pointless and all but hopeless mission?

It's a question translators often ask themselves. Those who attempt an answer are likely to say that some readers can indeed hear and appreciate the formal features of a translated poem and prize the opportunity to approach (if not replicate) the sensations experienced by readers of the poem in its native language. They will concede the more ominous points I have just enumerated, but they will observe, if they have given much thought to the subject, that all words are approximations of our thoughts and feelings, and that if the motivating ideas and emotions of the original poet can be intuited, then words can be found in the new language to approximate them while generating a music (meter and rhyme) similar if not identical to that of the reference poem. They will not deny that this is hard to do, that spectacular success is unlikely, but they embrace the challenge nonetheless.

Putting the problem in abstract terms, as I have just done, makes it sound somehow manageable. Confronting examples in actual poems shows it to be formidable. The difficulties fall into categories of ascending menace: *rhythmic resources, vocabulary or lexical resources,* and *nuance* or the problem of multiple meanings. I'll take these up successively.

Rhythmic Resources

Traditional English poetic meter is based on a fixed number of syllables and a fixed pattern of stresses in each line. The iambic pattern, our most common measure, is subject to complex variations that have been extensively analyzed.[1] Robert Frost oversimplified the matter but was substantially correct when he said English has virtually two meters: strict iambic and loose iambic, the latter admitting extra syllables and more variation in the placing of stresses. The standard classical line of English verse, the basis of Shakespeare's plays, Pope's satires, and Keats's sonnets, is iambic pentameter, a ten-syllable line of five iambic feet. Although Elizabethan poets experimented with "fourteeners" (lines of fourteen syllables or seven feet that, however, tended to fall into patterns of four plus three), very few English poems make use of six-foot lines, or hexameters, a line that Pope likened to a wounded snake.

French tradition, by contrast, gives pride of place to the twelve-syllable alexandrine. It is the line of Racine's, Corneille's, and Molière's plays and of most of the poems in Baudelaire's *Fleurs du mal*. However, the stress patterns of spoken French are much less emphatic than those of English or German, and they do not figure in French prosody. So the classical French line of twelve syllables undifferentiated by stress stands against the classical English line of ten syllables divided into five feet. Does this mean we must overstuff a pentameter line to fit in all the meaning of the corresponding alexandrine, or write six pentameter lines for five lines of classical French? Not necessarily. English is a somewhat more condensed language than French. A random piece of French prose, scrupulously translated, will often result in a somewhat shorter amount of English, a fact familiar to Canadians, who are accustomed to seeing the same material presented side by side in the two national languages.[2] These linguistic differences conspire to convince most translators to substitute iambic pentameter for the French alexandrine—and in fact on occasion (though not always) a French octosyllabic line can morph into an English trimeter:

Les Pas

Tes pas, enfants de mon silence,
Saintement, lentement placés,
Vers le lit de ma vigilance
Procèdent muets et glacés.
Personne pure, ombre divine,
Qu'ils sont doux, tes pas retenus !
Dieux ! . . . tous les dons que je devine
Viennent à moi sur ces pieds nus !
Si, de tes lèvres avancées,
Tu prépares pour l'apaiser,
À l'habitant de mes pensées
La nourriture d'un baiser,
Ne hâte pas cet acte tendre,
Douceur d'être et de n'être pas,
Car j'ai vécu de vous attendre,
Et mon cœur n'était que vos pas.

—Paul Valéry

Footsteps

Children of my silence,
Your saintly steps, unrushed,
Approach my pallet's vigil,
Frozen, timeless, hushed.
Pure one, divinest shadow,
Steps verging on retreat,
Gods—what gifts I envision
Borne on those naked feet!
If with lips pressed toward me
You deign to nourish this
Dweller in my obsessions
With an appeasing kiss,
Don't hasten to your mercy.
Being and not being is sweet.
My life is a vivid waiting,
My heart your padding feet.

(my translation)

So the metrical problem in not insuperable in the neighboring Indo-European languages. Spanish pays less attention to syllable count but still makes frequent use of a five-stress line, as does Italian. As does German, with an even more pronounced contrast between stressed and unstressed syllables. But in subtler ways these languages differ markedly. The great majority of words in Italian end with an unstressed syllable; therefore, the five-stress Italian verse line usually has such a syllable at the end—making it eleven syllables long: a hendecasyllable. In English verse such a line is said to have a feminine ending, and it occurs infrequently unless a poet takes care to employ such lines for their sonic effect (as in the odd-numbered lines of the poem just quoted). It would be all but impossible to create an English translation of the *Divine Comedy* that used feminine endings with the frequency of Dante's hendecasyllables.

German is closer to English in stress patterns,[3] but because German infinitives, declensional markers, and many plural affixes are unstressed, feminine endings are considerably more common in German verse than in English. It is possible to translate Goethe's *Faust* matching his lines rhyme for rhyme and meter for meter (including feminine endings), as Zsuzsanna Ozsváth and Frederick Turner have recently done, but it is not a project for the faint of heart:

Ihr Instrumente freilich spottet mein,
Mit Rad und Kämmen, Walz' und Bügel:
Ich stand am Tor, ihr solltet Schlüssel sein;
Zwar Euer Bart ist kraus, doch hebt ihr nicht die Riegel.
Geheimnisvoll am lichten Tag
Läßt sich Natur des Schleiers nicht berauben,
Und was sie deinem Geist nicht offenbaren mag,
Das swingst du ihr nicht ab mit Hebeln und mit Schrauben

You instruments, of course, now mock at me,
With wheel and clasp and reel and ratchet:
I'm at the gate, and you should be the key:
Your wards are bent and crumpled, and you won't unlatch it.
Demurest in the brightest day,
Nature won't let her veil be stolen ever,
And what your spirit can't reveal in its own way,
You cannot force with any jack, or any lever.

If a generalization can be drawn from these and other examples, it is that a translator cannot ignore the meter of the source poem but is not bound to reproduce it precisely in the second language. What is essential is that the meter chosen for the new version must be one that is easily perceived and feels natural to readers, most of whom will not know how the original poem sounded to its native audience.

Lexical Resources, Rhyme

When it comes to rhyme the difficulties multiply. Spanish and Italian boast large collections of words with matching endings, owing in part to tell-tale gender markings for masculine and feminine nouns and adjectives, and in part to verb forms that step in uniform fashion through the conjugations. As a result, it is only a bit of an exaggeration to say, with John Ciardi, that in Italian almost every word rhymes with every other.[4] With such a trove to work with, Dante could write some fourteen thousand lines in terza rima, a scheme relying on three instances of each rhyming sound. English does not have such resources. But it has others. In addition to the alternative of blank verse (forgoing rhyme altogether), or rhyming the first and last lines of each tercet, as Ciardi does, a translator can use half-rhyme, as Robert Pinsky does in his translation of the *Inferno*, to create a muted but still discernible sonic pattern that maintains the scheme of terza rima. This is a technique that can be helpful in many places, since it greatly increases the possibilities for rhyme regardless of the subject being dealt with.

> «Per più fïate li occhi ci sospinse
> quella lettura, e scolorocci il viso;
> ma solo un punto fu quel che ci vinse.
>
> Quando leggemmo il disïato riso
> esser basciato da cotanto amante,
> questi, che mai da me non fia diviso,
>
> la bocca mi basciò tutto tremante.
> Galeotto fu 'l libro e chi lo scrisse:
> quel giorno più non vi leggemmo avante.»

Mentre che l'uno spirto questo disse,
l'altro piangëa; sì che di pietade
io venni men così com' io morisse.

   —Dante, *Inferno,* canto 5

"Sometimes at what we read our glances joined,
Looking from the book each to the other's eyes,
And then the color in our faces drained.

But one particular moment alone it was
Defeated us: the longed-for smile, it said,
Was kissed by that most noble lover: at this,

This one, who now will never leave my side,
Kissed my mouth, trembling. A Galeotto, that book!
And so was he who wrote it; that day we read

No further." All the while the one shade spoke,
The other at her side was weeping; my pity
Overwhelmed me and I felt myself go slack.

   (translated by Robert Pinsky)

There are, however, instances where half-rhymes are not a satisfactory solution and true rhymes are not available. A notable example occurs in Rilke's famous sonnet "Archaic Torso of Apollo." The poem ends with an emphatic and surprising injunction: "Du musst dein Leben ändern." ("You must change your life.") The sentence is unambiguous and cannot be said differently. In the German original the final word *ändern* (change) forms a clear rhyme with the word *Rändern* (boundaries or margins) in the sonnet's twelfth line. But for *life* (unlike the Germans we must put our object after the verb), English has only a few possible rhymes to offer: *wife, strife, knife, fife, rife*—and none of them seem to fit with anything in the preceding lines of the poem. So, if the translator believes the highest priority is to keep the rhyme while accurately translating the unambiguous final sentence, the only option is to create a plausible context for one of those five possible words. Here's one possibility:

Wir kannten nicht sein unerhörtes Haupt,
darin die Augenäpfel reiften. Aber
sein Torso glüht noch wie ein Kandelaber,
in dem sein Schauen, nur zurückgeschraubt,

sich hält und glänzt. Sonst könnte nicht der Bug
der Brust dich blenden, und im leisen Drehen
der Lenden könnte nicht ein Lächeln gehen
zu jener Mitte, die die Zeugung trug.

Sonst stünde dieser Stein entstellt und kurz
unter der Schultern durchsichtigem Sturz
und flimmerte nicht so wie Raubtierfelle;

und bräche nicht aus allen seinen Rändern
aus wie ein Stern: denn da ist keine Stelle,
die dich nicht sieht. Du musst dein Leben ändern.

We never knew his unimagined head
in which the eyes were apples ripening,
and yet his torso radiates a ring
of light as if a now-dimmed streetlamp shed

a constant glow. How else could the convex
curve of his breast dazzle, and the soft turn
of loins become a smile you might discern
reaching that center that once bore his sex?

And how else could this stone, disfigured, scant
beneath the shoulders' smooth translucent slant,
still flicker like a momentary trace

of wolf's fur, burst its boundaries like the knife-
beams of a star? No, there is not a place
that doesn't see you. You must change your life.

(my translation)

The threatened violence of the predator in line eleven and the boundary-bursting star in line twelve comport with the visually evocative *knife-beams* phrase, but it is an invention, not a translation of any actual words in the German poem.

There is more to be said about this poem, much of which has been elaborated by William Gass in his book *Reading Rilke.*[5] The *Kandelaber* of the first stanza was likely a gas-fueled streetlamp, common in Rilke's time, which would have shed a cone of light on the street below. It could be dimmed by turning a screw-like mechanism, hence Rilke's odd-sounding term *zurückgeschraubt,* which means "screwed back" and provides a rhyme for *Haupt* (head) in the first line. Rilke himself was clearly not shy about bringing a remote, anachronistic reference into his poem about an ancient statue.

It is well to remember that poets who choose to write poems that rhyme, or poems that have rhyming elements, must be conscious of available rhymes at all times and must steer their argument, or their associations, toward expressions that will yield words that fit with other words they will also need. When Philip Larkin writes "Man hands on misery to man. / It deepens like a coastal shelf," he chooses that simile, ending on a word with very few English rhymes, because it will allow him to finish his poem with a bang: "Get out as early as you can / And don't have any kids yourself."[6] A translator wishing to put that verse into French or Russian will have the difficult task of finding a coastal reference and a pronominal intensifier that also happen to sound alike. This is why translation is hard or impossible, and why translators sometimes become inventive.

Nuance and Invention

Invention, a necessity within ill-defined limits, is a temptation for every translator. It is hardly possible to create a verse translation without some invention—sometimes of syntax, sometimes of vocabulary, sometimes of metaphor.[7] But occasionally a translator, obeying a mysterious impulse, begins to write essentially a new poem, though one that could not have existed without the original as inspiration and model. Consider this paraphrase of a sonnet by Jorge Luis Borges and its reinvention by Robert Mezey:

> On a certain street there is a certain solid door
> with its doorbell and its precise number
> and a taste of a lost paradise,
> which in the evening is not open

to my step. The journey done,
a longed-for voice once welcomed me
at the close of every day
into the peace of a loving night.
But no longer. My fate is otherwise:
the idle hours, the tainted memory,
the abuse of literature
and at the end an undesired death.
That stone is all I want. And all I ask:
those two abstract dates and oblivion.

On a certain street there is a certain door,
Unyielding, around which rockroses rise,
Charged with the scent of a lost paradise,
Which in the evening sunlight opens no more,
Or not to me. Once, in a better light,
Dearly awaited arms would wait for me
And in the impatient fading of the day
The joy and peace of the embracing night.
No more of that. Now, a day breaks and dies,
Releasing empty hours and impure
Fantasies, and the abuse of literature,
The lawless images and artful lies,
And pointless tears, and the envy of other men.
And then the longing for oblivion.[8]

The inventions begin in the second line. Borges mentions a door with a bell and a precise number. The idea of a *precise* number may have been intended to contrast with the "abstract dates" (of birth and death) on the tombstone in the last lines. Perhaps feeling a house number could scarcely be anything but precise, and perhaps already planning to change the ending of the poem, Mezey introduces something completely new: the rockroses, which lend to the scene an air of charm and domesticity soon to be revealed as an illusion. After that he largely follows Borges (except for the phrase "a day breaks and dies") until the last three lines. Then, where Borges looks toward an unhappy death, desiring only a stone with its "abstract" (meaningless) dates and oblivion, Mezey elaborates on the "abuse of literature," with "lawless images and artful lies," and blends that self-accusation with the despair of the rejected lover or spouse: the "pointless tears," the "envy of other men," and the "longing for oblivion."

Mezey has created a very successful poem which, however, departs significantly from its model. Where for Borges death is unwanted (*no gustada*) but oblivion is requested, Mezey enumerates the abandoned lover's torments (vain tears and envy) and actively longs for erasure. Is it a translation or a new invention? To his credit, Mezey labels it simply "After Borges."

Sometimes the invention takes place at third hand. Two generations ago, Yvor Winters translated Baudelaire's poem "Le Squelette Laboureur" ("Skeletons Digging"). Here are the first two stanzas of Part II:

De ce terrain que vous fouillez,	Out of the earth at which you spade,
Manants résignés de funèbres,	Funereal laborers, tired and done,
De tout l'effort de vos vertèbres.	Out of your straining naked bone,
Ou de vos muscles dépouillés,	Out of your muscles bare and frayed,
Dites, quelle moisson étrange,	Tell me, what harvest do you win?
Forçats arrachés au charnier,	Slaves snatched from the charnel ground,
Tirez-vous, et de quel fermier	Who is the farmer drives this round
Avez-vous à remplir la grange?	To fill his barn? And what your sin?

Note a small detail: where Baudelaire began two lines with the preposition *de* (and it occurs again as the second word of line four), Winters used a corresponding prepositional phrase (*out of*) at the start of three lines. That repetition starts to create an incantatory, hypnotic effect in the poem. The translation was included in a volume of Baudelaire's poems in English, published by Marthiel and Jackson Matthews in 1955.[9] It might have been forgotten in a few years. But not long afterward the young Philip Levine came to Stanford to study with Winters, and a few years later he wrote a poem that begins:

Out of burlap sacks, out of bearing butter,
Out of black bean and wet slate bread,
Out of the acids of rage, the candor of tar,
Out of creosote, gasoline, drive shafts, wooden dollies,
They Lion grow.
. . .

Out of the bones' need to sharpen and the muscles' to stretch,
They Lion grow.

. . .

                  from the reeds of shovels,
The grained arm that pulls the hands,
They Lion grow.

This poem is, of course, "They Feed They Lion," probably the most widely read poem Levine wrote in his career. In no way is it a translation of Baudelaire or anyone else. We don't know if Levine was consciously thinking of the Baudelaire translation as he composed it. Yet the genetic traces of the earlier poem are unmistakable. The repeated phrase and the references to the bones and the muscles of the diggers suggest a set of rhythms and images that must have lodged deep in the young poet's mind.

A careful look at the Baudelaire poem will reveal that the translator has chosen particular English meanings for words like *manants* and *forçats*—and not the most likely at that—from among multiple possibilities offered by French usage, tradition, and etymology. (Both are words used much less often nowadays than in Baudelaire's time.) Selection is necessary, since the congeries of meanings associated with a word in one language is unlikely to be matched by a similar set in another language. But the need to choose among possibilities allows, or forces, the translator to direct the poem into certain areas of meaning, and away from others, all of which may be hovering in the aura of associations brought mindfully to the poem by its creator.

Even though many English words derive from Latin, speakers of French live much closer to the Latin origins of their words than English speakers do. Most of us, if we call someone *supercilious*, do not visualize a raised eyebrow (*super*, "above" + *cilium*, "eyelid"), but Paul Valéry did. In his poem "Le Cimetière marin" ("The Graveyard by the Sea") he writes of

Eau sourcilleuse, Œil qui gardes en toi
Tant de sommeil sous un voile de flamme

And the supercilious water, seen as an eye that keeps so much sleep to itself under a veil of flame, clearly calls forth for French readers the image of the haughty raised eyebrow. How to bring that visual immediacy to the minds of English readers encountering the passage in translation? The word "supercilious" has no immediate physical connotations for us. We may, however, associate an eye with the word "arch," a word that means "characterized by clever or sly alertness," according to Merriam-Webster, which cites Jane Austen: "that arch eye of yours! it sees through everything." We may even imagine an arched eyebrow, although "arch" in this sense probably derives from a root meaning "main" or "principal." So when I came to translate Valéry's lines I settled on:

> arch waters, great Eye keeping to yourself
> vast stores of sleep beneath a veil of flame[10]

Many words in every language have overtones: secondary meanings or associations that may lie hidden and unnoticed until a poet provides a context that brings them to mind. The translator is obliged to search in the second language for words with similar overtones. But "similar" is the best we can do. Each language has its own history, and each word its associations, correspondences, and preferred company. To make some overtones perceptible in the target language is inevitably to ignore or obscure others that may have been part of the original poet's elaborate design but are unavailable in the new linguistic environment.

Many of these problems arise to perplex the translator of an early poem of Rilke's:

> Vielleicht, daß ich durch schwere Berge gehe
> in harten Adern, wie ein Erz allein;
> und bin so tief, daß ich kein Ende sehe
> und keine Ferne: alles wurde Nähe
> und alle Nähe wurde Stein.
>
> Ich bin ja noch kein Wissender im Wehe,—
> so macht mich dieses große Dunkel klein;
> bist Du es aber: mach dich schwer, brich ein:
> daß deine ganze Hand an mir geschehe
> und ich an dir mit meinem ganzen Schrein.

Perhaps [it's true] that I'm passing through heavy
mountains, in hard veins like ore alone; and I am so
deep that I can see no end and no distance:
everything grows near and all nearness becomes
stone.

I am as yet no expert at pain, so this great darkness
makes me small; but if You are [expert], make
yourself heavy, break in, so that your whole hand
happens to me and I to you with my entire cry.

—from *The Book of Hours (Das Stundenbuch)*[11]

I am giving only a literal prose translation of this poem to start, because
there are many issues to be resolved in arriving at a verse translation. For the
translator, most of the problems come in the second stanza. Rilke's phrase *kein
Wissender im Wehe* is not idiomatic modern German. It is understandable, but
it sounds oddly archaic. Literally it means "no knower in pain." A translation
that captures the archaism and the sense together might be "I am not yet a
witting one of pain." While this locution has the virtue of imitating Rilke's
alliteration, it brings the English-speaking reader up short with a strange-
sounding expression that is slightly weaker in its impact than the single word
Wissender in German.

An even greater difficulty occurs in the poem's last line—in fact in its last
word. At the most obvious level, *Schrein* is a contraction of *Schreien*, which
means "to cry" or in its nominative form "crying" or "a cry." But a *Schrein*
in German is also a cabinet (a confined space) or a shrine. And the word
also means "coffin." So with that one word Rilke has conjured up weeping or
pleading, confinement, religious memorial, and death. Any translation will
inevitably be a stripped-down version, preserving the essential denotation of
the poem but unable to evoke the subliminal associations that give it special
resonance for German-speaking readers. Here is my best attempt:

These must be mountains I pass through alone,
embedded in hard veins like so much ore,
and I'm so deep I see no end in store,

no distance either; everything is near
and all the nearness solid stone.

I am not yet a witting sage of pain,
so this great darkness only makes me small;
But if You are, grow heavy and break in:
that your whole hand upon me may befall
and I on you with cries I can't restrain.

In English, the first line of the second stanza has a slightly formal if not archaic air; the word "befall" in the penultimate line is a good match for the German *geschehe* ("happen"): similarly strange without seeming impossibly weird; and the last line conveys the primary meaning but forgoes the secondary ones (except for the notion of restraint) that make the line reverberate in the minds of German readers.

■ ■ ■ ■ ■

Poets vary considerably in the degree to which they select words with multiple meanings and invest their poems with language-dependent implications and connotations. All things being equal (as they rarely are), poems relying on straightforward denotative meanings will be easier to translate than poems with multilayered meanings that are suggestive rather than explicit. The latter call for more invention on the part of the translator, who can rarely aspire to word-for-word or even thought-for-thought equivalence. Ideally the translator will be a poet in his own right, with a wide-ranging linguistic imagination and a kind of fearlessness likely to evoke the scorn of pedants and the delight of readers. If he or she is blessed as well with a superb ear, the result may be a poem that achieves a second life in its new language.

NOTES

1. See, e.g., Morris Halle and Samuel Jay Keyser, "Illustration and Defense of a Theory of the Iambic Pentameter," *College English* 33:2 (1971), 154–76; and Grosvenor Powell, "The Two Paradigms for Iambic Pentameter and Twentieth-Century Metrical Experimentation," *Modern Language Review* 91:3 (1996), 561–77.

2. In a set of instructions accompanying an outdoor table umbrella I received recently, the English version consists of sixty-one words, the French version eighty-two.

3. But particular constructions can play havoc for the translator, especially with poems that have been set to music. Heine's poem "Der Tod, das ist die kühle Nacht" is an example. German places a definite article before "death"; English does not. We could say, "Death is the long cool night" (adding a word to fit the meter). But that still gives us only six syllables, and Heine's poem has eight here. Singers who perform Brahms's setting of the poem are well advised to stay with the German original.

4. See Dante, *The Inferno*, trans. John Ciardi (Signet, 2009), translator's note, p. x.

5. William H. Gass, *Reading Rilke: Reflections on the Problems of Translation* (Knopf, 1999).

6. Philip Larkin, "This Be the Verse," *Collected Poems* (Farrar, Straus, 1989).

7. As Richard Wilbur put it in an interview with Peter Davison, "I don't want to concede to any freer translator that he more perfectly captures the spirit of the original. I do try to get the spirit—a thought-for-thought fidelity to the original. To seek for word-for-word fidelity is nonsense, but thought-for-thought fidelity is possible. I also try to find and keep to a parallel form. I try to be as slavish as is consistent with being imaginative and lively." *Atlantic Monthly*, September 1999.

8. "N.W." from Robert Mezey, *Collected Poems, 1952–1999* (University of Arkansas Press, 2000), based on "H.O." from Jorge Luis Borges, *Poemas del Alma* in *Poesia completa* (Vintage español, 2012).

9. Charles Baudelaire, *Flowers of Evil,* selected and edited by Marthiel and Jackson Mathews (New Directions, 1955; rev. 1989).

10. Paul Valéry, "The Graveyard by the Sea," translated by Jan Schreiber, *Literary Imagination* 9:1 (2007), reprinted in *The Poems of Paul Valéry* (Cambridge Scholars, 2021).

11. We can get a good sense of another poet's reaction to this piece from Louise Bogan. Writing to Theodore Roethke in 1935, she observes that in this poem, "you get a magnificent single poetic concept carried through with perfect ease, because it is thoroughly informed by passion. . . . Rilke is terribly upset about his inability to get away from it all—you know that without my telling you, but let me maunder on. So he starts to write a poem, and he turns the lack of freedom into a perfectly frightful metaphor: he is unable to see any distance, any horizon (lovely word!), and he is so unable to see that he feels himself inside a mountain, like a vein of ore. Everything is nearness, and all the nearness stone. Magnificent. And then what happens? Well, he can't stand it, so he turns to someone for help, and he drags the person into the metaphor. I am not adept at pain, he says, but if you are, make yourself heavy (isn't that schwer wonderful?) and break in, so that your whole hand may fall upon me and I on you with my whole cry. . . . Now a poem like that cannot be written by technique alone. It is carved out of agony, just as a statue is carved out of marble. And you must let yourself suffer, once in a while, lovey, in order that you may do same." Letter to Theodore Roethke, August 23, 1935, in Ruth Limmer, ed., *What the Woman Lived* (Harcourt, 1973).

III. MAPS OF DIFFICULT TERRAIN

9

SERPENT IN THE TREE
Poetry of a Fallen World

Horseness is the whatness of allhorse.

—James Joyce, *Ulysses*

From an infant's first rejection of a proffered spoon, dissatisfaction is probably the most common and most universal human response to the world. Small wonder that attempts at systematic thought often start by noting the gulf between what we can imagine and what we find before us. Justification for this disdain for the phenomenal world, the one we perceive with our senses, goes back at least to Plato. Our ability to imagine an ideal entails a reciprocal awareness that any particular exemplar fails in some respect to measure up. For Plato, in Albert Stöckl's summary,

> Ideas alone have real being; they alone are perfect, unchangeable, enduring, eternal, imperishable. Unchanging in itself, the ideal world moves in viewless majesty above the world of phenomena, representing within itself the full perfection of Being. The phenomenal world, on the other hand, is the sphere of imperfection, of change, of transition, the region where things exist in time, and begin to be. . . . Nothing ever attains perfection, for at each moment things cease to be what they were a moment before. All things are at the transition point from Being to Non-being, and from Non-being to Being; they are, and are not, at the same time. It follows that there can be no question here of Being in its perfection.[1]

The Scholastics found this line of thought readily adaptable to a theological setting. God represented the perfection of being; creation, on the other hand, manifested a lesser kind. The perfection of the universe, according to Aquinas, "requires that there should be some [beings] which can fail in goodness and which sometimes do fail."[2] This modification—or rationalization—would become the prevailing theology, surviving even the Reformation, upon which Milton would build the edifice of *Paradise Lost.*

But an even more radical idea had long lurked in the background. Preceding the Scholastics by many centuries, the Gnostic heresy maintained that "the blame for the world's failings lies not with humans, but with the creator."[3] To put it crudely, the creator (the Demiurge) had bungled the job, and our present deprivations are a direct result.

That heresy was long suppressed, but once the grip of established religion was loosened, the Gnostic idea became a fertile ground for poets. J. V. Cunningham offers a characteristically unadorned summary of the issue, couched in the language of morality, rather than theology, in his poem "Haecceity":

> Evil is any this or this
> Pursued beyond hypothesis.
>
> It is the scribbling of affection
> On the blank pages of perfection.
>
> Evil is presentness bereaved
> Of all the futures it conceived,
>
> Willful and realized restriction
> Of the insatiate forms of fiction.
>
> It is this poem, or this act.
> It is this absolute of fact.

The argument now, as set forth here by a lapsed Catholic, gives a moral coloration to the philosophical reasoning. In Cunningham's extreme formulation, any actuality at all is not only flawed but morally abhorrent. Taken seriously the doctrine would suggest that total obliteration of the physical world is the only cure for the evil of existence. The poem is a provocative intellectual exercise but hardly, one would hope, a program.

Nevertheless, the radical disparity between the known reality and the imagined ideal has proved a powerful motive for many poems, particularly when it can be expressed in terms of a plausible human situation. Innumerable sonnets have played on the notion of the love object as unattainable ideal—or the lover who is all too human and therefore far from the ideal. Philip Sidney clearly expected a negative answer when he asked, "Hath this world aught so fair as Stella is?" but in Sonnet 141 Shakespeare addresses his unideal lover frankly: "In faith, I do not love thee with mine eyes / For they in thee a thousand errors note." He goes on to conclude that love steers not by the senses but by the admittedly foolish heart.

Far more comprehensive, philosophically, is a recasting of the Genesis myth of the "fall" as an attempt to deal with a fatally flawed universe. This was the approach of Paul Valéry in "Ébauche d'un serpent." The poem's narrator is the Serpent of the title, who shares with Milton's Satan a ferocious antagonism toward the creator, stemming in part from jealousy and a sense of unjust personal deprivation. Valéry's Serpent, however, has a more elaborate rationale for his resentments, one closely resembling the Gnostic scheme. In the poem that comprises his extended monologue, he tells us with a kind of intellectual disdain that God erred in creating the universe out of nothing, because actual being is inevitably flawed.

> Bored by his pure tableau,
> God became He who mars
> His own perfection. Hence
> He saw his Principle
> Dispersed in consequence,
> His Unity in stars.[4]

These lines demonstrate Valéry's remarkable ability to combine abstract thought with a visceral awareness of the phenomenal world. "Principle" dispersed in "consequence" is a completely abstract notion; but "unity" dispersed in "stars" is suddenly concrete and vivid, as well as consistent with contemporary scientific understanding of the origins of the universe.

In particular (to continue the argument), human beings are far from the perfection of their creator; in the Serpent's telling God projects his sense of failure onto his newly formed creatures. "Look deeply in my shade," the Serpent admonishes:

> Your tragic image there,
> The pride of my dark mirror,
> So tortured you, the air
> You breathed upon the clay
> Was your sigh of despair.

Valéry is fond of the notion that light is visible only in relation to darkness—a notion treated more extensively in his other great poem, "Le Cimetière marin." The Serpent vaunts himself as the means by which God, who is all light, can see his own image and thereby recognize his error.

It is worthwhile to pause at this point and consider the vast philosophical gulf between the narrative Valéry sets forth and the traditional Christian legend as articulated by Milton in *Paradise Lost*. Milton's story is based on an ancient, simple concept of justice: when an offense is committed—particularly an offense by a subordinate against a superior—there must be a reprisal. So the offense of disobedience (eating the fruit of the forbidden tree) calls for a punishment seemingly far in excess of the transgression: not only the offenders are to be punished, but all their offspring in perpetuity. Thus all mankind is contaminated by the original sin of its progenitors.

But in Christian theology there is a loophole. The ancient practice of sacrifice may be invoked to allow a symbolic victim to step forward and bear the punishment incurred by the offenders. Here is the crucial passage in *Paradise Lost*. God is the speaker:

> Man disobeying,
> Disloyal breaks his fealtie, and sinns
> Against the high Supremacie of Heav'n,
> Affecting God-head, and so loosing all,
> To expiate his Treason hath naught left,
> But to destruction sacred and devote,
> He with his whole posteritie must dye,

Dye hee or Justice must; unless for him
Som other able, and as willing, pay
The rigid satisfaction, death for death.[5]

Milton's universe is not the result of God's error. Its seeming imperfections (human and angelic fallibility) are rather part of the divine plan:

Not free, what proof could they have givn sincere
Of true allegiance, constant Faith or Love,
Where onely what they needs must do, appear,
Not what they would?[6]

Milton's God, it seems, requires sincere, freely made expressions of adoration and voluntary conformity, and he will visit eternal damnation on those who fail to comply. The mills of justice grind without pity—unless a suitable sacrificial victim bears the punishment on mankind's behalf. Christian doctrine generally stipulates further that the sacrifice (i.e. Christ's crucifixion) has its desired effect only on those individuals who repent and have faith in the resurrected Christ.

Far from exemplifying the grand plan of Milton's vision, Valéry's universe, as characterized by his Serpent, is closer to the Gnostic conception: it is the flawed product of a cosmic mistake. There is no rectifying it, because it has departed fatally and finally from the ideal state of unrealized potentiality. Awareness of this degraded condition evokes in the Serpent equal parts of sadness and abhorrence, made more acute by chagrin that he himself has not been accorded the preeminence he feels is his due.

But the first breath of his Word
Was ME! The grandest star
The mad creator spoke.
I am! I shall be! I
Light up his waning sky
With the Seducer's fire!

God's error extends to and is compounded by the newly created human beings. They offend the Serpent by their complacent stupidity as well as by their favored position in the order of creation. Out of resentment and a desire for revenge, he resolves to instill in these malleable creatures his own restless passion for knowledge—and thus to challenge, through them, the primacy of his silent and seemingly imperturbable divine rival. He addresses the new interlopers:

Made in that loathed image!
I hate you as I hate
The Name that would create
All these flawed prodigies.
I'm He who modifies;
I retouch trusting hearts
With sure, mysterious sense.
We'll change these flaccid works,
These slippery garden snakes,
To reptiles of revenge!

His method will employ verbal persuasion, following the model of a sexual seduction and utilizing both acute psychological probity and deftly deployed rhetoric. In a series of remarkable stanzas he works slowly on the impressionable Eve, flattering her and dropping subtle temptations in "The downy labyrinth / Of that amazing ear."

"Nothing's less sure," I breathed,
"Than God's pronouncement, Eve.
Live knowledge must exceed
The enormity of this fruit.
Ignore the old Absolute
Who cursed the smallest bite.
But should your mouth conceive
A thirst that longs to receive
This half-withheld delight—
All time's dissolved here, Eve!"

The object of this rhetoric is not the "fall" or corruption of mankind—since human beings are represented as deeply flawed to begin with—but the instillation of an insatiable thirst to know everything that can be known. And Eve, therefore, is not merely a weak vessel serving as a conduit to Adam; she is about to be the first human being to be seized by an intellectual passion.

However, we do not see her in the throes of that passion; she occupies our attention only while attending to the Serpent's allurements:

> An eyelid struck the silence—
> But breath swelled the dark breast
> That the Tree's shade possessed.
> The other shone like a pistil.
> —Hiss, hiss! it sang to me.
> And I felt energy
> Run through my whip. The thrill
> In every cumbering coil
> Vibrated from the beryl
> Of my crest out toward peril!

While we infer a mounting interest on Eve's part, we have little doubt that the Serpent himself is sexually aroused. To our contemplation of the ironies in the prescription of intellectual craving as a response to a flawed universe made by an all-knowing creator, the poem thus adds a moiety of Gallic sexual titillation.

Eve, of course, finally succumbs, and the Serpent experiences—and witnesses—a moment of almost orgasmic triumph—

> Delighting in temptation,
> Yield to the lures you see.
> Let thirst for transformation
> Ring the Forbidden Tree
> Round with a chain of poses.
> Come without coming! Step
> Vaguely, heavy with roses.
> Dear body, dance and forget!
> Here pleasure's sole decree
> Justifies what will be.

—followed by the inevitable regret:

O foolish to indulge
This sterile dalliance;
To see the long back quake
In disobedience . . .

But Valéry's Serpent, despite his implacable resentment toward God, acts out of a motive more evidently rational than Milton's Satan, who expressed a commitment to Evil in all its forms and yet—in one of his most human moments—from a welter of conflicting feelings proclaimed, "My self am Hell."[7] If the Serpent indeed wishes to torment mankind with an unappeasable thirst, it is a thirst for knowledge that can help the seeker address the deficiencies in his being. A trio of stanzas near the end of the poem comprises an unabashed paean to the Tree of Knowledge, seen as striving endlessly toward an unattainable ideal:

Press back the infinite
Marked by your rising crest,
And know yourself to be
All Knowledge, grave to nest!

Since the poem from the beginning has been narrated in the Serpent's voice, these stanzas must also be understood as spoken by him. On the other hand, there is no reason to believe their sentiments are not also Valéry's own. The workings of the mind, and knowledge of all kinds, were at the center of the poet's concerns for his entire life.

Such knowledge, of course, is not necessarily gratifying. The Serpent's glare shakes loose from the tree "the fruits of death, / Disorder, and despair." These too are facts of the human condition. Nevertheless, the poem ends ambiguously: the Serpent sounds a note of triumph, saying he is repaid by seeing "Huge hopes of bitter fruit / Madden the heirs of flesh." But in the concluding lines he also announces:

Their thirst exalts toward Being
The strange and absolute
Power of Nothingness.

(Jusqu'à l'Être exalte l'étrange / Toute-Puissance du Néant!). If, that is, the created universe is at best a degraded form of Being, perhaps the pursuit of knowledge is a pursuit of a more complete Being and thus an enhancement, or exaltation, of the power of the original Nothingness out of which it was formed.[8] Or is Nothingness the end of all? Is the Serpent, in the guise of a savage nihilism, offering in a veiled form an optimistic, albeit long-range, vision of human destiny? Or is he telling us that the pursuit of knowledge will lead humanity nowhere and that the void will triumph?

The obligation to avoid ambiguity weighs far lighter on the poet than on the philosopher.

In contrast to the dynamic and vengeful God of *Paradise Lost,* Valéry's God remains silent and inscrutable in the face of the Serpent's—and Eve's—provocation. There is no edict, no pronouncement, no banishment. It seems we will have to wait and see whether the radical plan to give human beings access to the secret mechanisms of the universe has improved their lot or sealed their doom. The jury, one might say, is still out.

Clearly the idea of existence as essentially evil, or at least a radical degradation, is a fraught one; the human fondness for existence (what else do we have, after all?) generates a natural sympathy for those who embrace or exploit it. Blake said that Milton, because he was a true poet, was of the devil's party without knowing it. Old Nick has often seemed the sort of fellow one could have a friendly conversation with. Goethe in *Faust* has Mephistopheles chat with God and afterwards remark, "It's very pretty of such a great gentleman to speak so humanly with the devil himself."[9] And Valéry's Serpent, whose impatience with mankind's limitations many of us can share, seems an urbane and clever creature who may even have our long-range interests at heart.

As confidence in a scientific model based on testable hypotheses began to outstrip faith in religious rationales, the presumed gulf between the ideal and the actual began to seem less troublesome. Of course actuality differed from ideal mathematical perfection: the difference could even be quantified. If a component could be machined to small enough tolerances, it could fulfill its purpose elegantly, however minutely it might deviate from the theoretical norm. Imperfection, a fact of life, was real but it could be managed.

Similarly, a government of checks and balances could, it was believed (or hoped), counter or elide such flaws as zealotry, fanaticism, and the inevitable human lust for power. The old religious concept of sin[10] was replaced by various identifiable and treatable pathologies. Human institutions, imperfect as they were, served as the best bulwark against barbarism and anarchy. The time-honored elaborate system of unimaginable rewards and all-too-readily imaginable punishments dramatized by Dante moved in our collective consciousness from the nonfiction to the fiction category.

It took W. H. Auden, working from a human model practically before his eyes, to give us, in "Danse Macabre," a truly frightening representation of evil at work in a debased world. In such a place the vestiges of elegance and culture are stripped away:

> It's farewell to the drawing-room's mannerly cry,
> The professor's logical whereto and why,
> The frock-coated diplomat's polished aplomb,
> Now matters are settled with gas and with bomb.

Although the traditional figure of the devil is invoked in this poem, Auden makes no further reference to the apparatus of Judeo-Christian myth (God, heaven and hell, temptation and fall). The ideal state, of which our world is traditionally seen as a degradation, is treated not as a metaphysical concept on a par with Plato's Forms, Aquinas's Heaven, or Milton's prelapsarian Eden, but as the civilized and sheltered milieu of the educated class:

> The works for two pianos, the brilliant stories
> Of reasonable giants and remarkable fairies,
> The pictures, the ointments, the frangible wares
> And the branches of olive are stored upstairs.

And that seemingly impregnable milieu is intruded on by, of all things, the figures of an all-but-forgotten morality play:

> For the Devil has broken parole and arisen,
> He has dynamited his way out of prison,
> Out of the well where his Papa throws
> The rebel angel, the outcast rose.

Even stately iambic rhythms are jettisoned; the poem proceeds at an anapestic gallop to develop a picture of a world in the clutches of a psychopath.
And unlike Valéry's Serpent, this devil has no interest in "retouching" human
beings; he seeks only to destroy them.

O were he to triumph, dear heart, you know
To what depths of shame he would drag you low;
He would steal you away from me, yes, my dear,
He would steal you and cut off your beautiful hair.

Partway through the poem, a self-described Devil-chaser emerges as narrator, but the result for humanity is equally dire:

For me it is written the Devil to chase
And to rid the earth of the human race.
. . .
I must take charge of the liquid fire
And storm the cities of human desire.

The destroyer is a monster of ego with no interest in humanity.

I shall ride the parade in a platinum car,
My features will shine, my name will be Star,
Day-long and night-long the bells I shall peal,
And down the long street I shall turn the cartwheel.

The end times are upon all, and none will be saved, for humanity is part of
the problem:

For it's order and trumpet and anger and drum
And power and glory command you to come;
The graves shall fly open and let you all in,
And the earth shall be emptied of mortal sin.

The poem was written in 1937—fifteen years after the publication of Valéry's
poem—as, with the Spanish civil war and the German invasion of the Rhine-

land, Auden foresaw Europe being engulfed by war and a rapacious dictatorship. It required no leap of imagination to see the actual world as a hideously deformed reflection of the ideal. Wholesale destruction was already widespread, and all that people held dear would be shortly put to the sword.

> The fishes are silent deep in the sea,
> The skies are lit up like a Christmas tree,
> The star in the West shoots its warning cry:
> "Mankind is alive, but Mankind must die."
>
> So good-bye to the house with its wallpaper red,
> Good-bye to the sheets on the warm double bed,
> Good-bye the beautiful birds on the wall,
> It's good-bye, dear heart, good-bye to you all.

Auden's poem can be seen as a direct descendant of Valéry's,[11] but it is equally effective when read with no knowledge of its French predecessor. It does not depend on our familiarity with a philosophical framework that views the world of the senses as a degradation of the ideal, even though it does employ a stock figure (the devil) of traditional Christianity. Its success lies in its ability to tie the ancient and to many people no longer quite credible apparatus of that religion to the undeniable facts playing out on the pages of the newspapers.

To summarize: the ancient problem of the disjunction between the ideal and the actual—a problem that some see as deriving from a linguistic confusion between a type (signified by a word) and any particular instance of the type (often signified by the same word)—has long been cast in moral and religious terms and re-expressed as an earthly degradation of heavenly perfection. We have seen the problem dealt with in three ways, depending on how fault is assigned:

1. Milton's universe: Human beings are responsible for their own fall, though they were led by Satan to violate a divine commandment. The only hope is to repent and believe.
2. Valéry's universe: God is responsible for the flawed world and flawed humanity. The Serpent uses Eve as a means of revenge, giving her (and Adam)

an unquenchable lust for knowledge by which they aspire to rival their creator. It is not clear how that works out for mankind.

3. Auden's universe: The force of evil in human form is responsible for the imminent destruction of all we hold dear. No remedy is proposed.

A single philosophical premise lies behind all three poems, but the conclusions drawn, and the modes of argument and imagery by which they are reached, are as different as were the poets' motivations in writing them. Poetry may make use of a philosophical or religious framework at times, just as it may make use of a myth or legend, for its human meaning and the emotional power that can be drawn from presenting the component details with imagination and artistry. But in our day a poet rarely aims to elaborate a philosophical argument in the medium of verse. Rather the human implications of the premise develop out of a lifetime of perceptive observation and reflection. Inevitably, then, the poem becomes a form of prophecy—both a moral pronouncement and a foretelling—which may amount to a warning.

That the foretelling and the warning may be ambiguous should not surprise us. The point of a cautionary message is that the dire future might be otherwise, if only we will take heed. And the unresolvable question is at what point the feared outcome becomes inevitable and the prophecy bends toward tragedy.

NOTES

1. Albert Stöckl, *Handbook of the History of Philosophy, Part I: Pre-Scholastic Philosophy* (Leopold Classical Library, 2016), 76.

2. *Summa Theologica* I, Q48, 2.

3. Stephan A. Hoeller, "The Cosmos," *The Gnosis Archive* (http://gnosis.org/gnintro.htm), accessed 7/6/2024.

4. "Sketch of a Serpent," my translation, *Hudson Review*, 29:1 (1976), 9–17. All other quotations of this poem are from the same source. The French original is in octosyllabic verse; the English version is in iambic trimeter, which to my ear retains the quickness and lightness of the French poem while sacrificing very little content. Facing-page presentations of Valéry's poem and my English version are printed in my book *The Poems of Paul Valéry* (2021).

5. III, 203–212. Adam and Eve, of course, have caused no death, but their mortal punishment is decreed by God, who then announces that their actual and immediate death can be stayed only if another agrees to die in their place.

6. III, 103–106.

7. IV, 75. See a related discussion in chapter 11.

8. This may be once again a restatement of contemporary theories of the origin of our universe. But of course in the scheme of the poem the creation of being out of nothingness recapitulates the original fault that the Serpent protested from the outset. His own machinations thus threaten to trap him in an endless repetitive cycle.

9. "Es ist gar hübsch von einem grossen Herrn / So menschlich mit dem Teufel selbst zu sprechen." Prologue to *Faust*, part I.

10. As still recognized with psychological acuity by Robert Bridges in "Low Barometer":

> And Reason kens he herits in
> A haunted house. Tenants unknown
> Assert their squalid lease of sin
> With earlier title than his own.
>
> Unbodied presences, the pack'd
> Pollution and remorse of Time,
> Slipp'd from oblivion reënact
> The horrors of unhouseld crime.

11. See W. H. Auden, "Valéry: l'Homme d'esprit," *Hudson Review*, 22:3 (1969), 425–32.

10

THE CURATOR AS ORACLE

A Guide to *The Harlem Gallery*

Writers and scholars may feel more potential solace in speaking about art that's clearly invested in racial uplift than they do in unpacking a kind of existential conundrum that demands a great deal more of its viewer and denies the relief of a comforting directive.

> —Megan O'Grady, "Once Overlooked, Black Abstract Painters Are Finally Given Their Due," *New York Times*, 2/12/21

Melvin Tolson, a significant poet of the twentieth century, is not as widely known as he should be, and even where he is known he is not widely read. His writing is admittedly difficult, but it rewards careful study. Our historical moment, with its renewed focus on once-neglected Black writers, is an optimal time to acquaint ourselves with this poet, who has a great deal to say about how to *see* and how to *read*.

Tolson was born in 1898 in Moberly, Missouri. He graduated from Lincoln University and taught for many years at Wiley College in Texas. (His success there as a debate coach was chronicled in the 2007 film *The Great Debaters*.) He later taught at Langston University in Oklahoma. His epic poem *Libretto for the Republic of Liberia* (1953) is considered a major modernist work.

Published in 1964, *The Harlem Gallery*, his last major work, is a book-length poem in twenty-four parts, one for each letter of the Greek alphabet, that creates a fictional world—a combination art gallery and nightclub in Harlem—in which the nature of art, and the ways of producing, perceiving, and judging it, are anatomized, as Tolson would say, to a fare-thee-well. The primary narrative voice in the poem is that of the Curator, the man in charge of the gallery, the one who chooses the paintings it displays. While finely attuned to art, the Curator makes no claim to be an artist himself. But numerous artists seize our attention, representing music and poetry as well as painting, and their arguments and pronouncements comprise a running interdisciplinary exchange on questions of aesthetics, personal identity, and achievement.

Presented in a dense, allusive, highly metaphorical and often ambiguous language, studded with references to obscure historical persons, places, and events, in a kind of parody of the high modernism associated with Eliot and Pound, Tolson's poem offers a forbidding surface that has undoubtedly deterred far too many readers over the more than fifty years since it was published. This is unfortunate, because the poem speaks directly to many of the issues of judgment that poets and critical readers of poetry wrestle with every day. For a sense of the poem's prickly texture, consider the opening lines (which, like all the metrically varied lines in the book, are centered):

> The Harlem Gallery, an Afric pepper bird,
> awakes me at a people's dusk of dawn.
> The age altars its image, a dog's hind leg,
> and hazards the moment of truth in pawn.

From Raymond Nelson's helpful notes in the 1999 edition of Tolson's poems,[1] we learn that a pepper bird is a type of African hornbill that can be noisy. We also are reminded that *Dusk of Dawn* was the title of a 1940 autobiographical text by W. E. B. Du Bois dealing with race relations. The third line tells us that the age worships its own image ("altars" is not a typo but a pun), which may be crooked, bent, or distorted; and the fourth line suggests that we risk or bet everything on what we believe to be true. Clearly the poem, with its far-flung references and allusions, will call for close and patient reading throughout. But it will also offer frequent rewards. A page later we come upon these poignant lines:

> but often I hear a dry husk-of-locust blues
> descending the tone ladder of a laughing goose,
> syncopating between

the faggot and the noose:
"Black Boy, O Black Boy,
is the port worth the cruise?"

The fictional setting of the poem—an art gallery in a nightclub patronized by working people and intellectuals, artists and pretenders, tipplers, hustlers, and sober citizens—offers a canvas on which to represent the complex life and mores of Harlem's largely Black community, and in the process to debate the nature of art (what it is, what it does) and the role of the artist in shaping and extending that community.

In what follows I want to trace that argument as it evolves through the scenes of Tolson's human comedy. It will be necessary to pass by many of the poet's recondite images, metaphors, and allusions, but by placing emphasis on the main critical discussion that winds through the text, I hope to help readers find their way more surely through a dense and distracting landscape.

■ ■ ■ ■

In the first canto, Alpha, the Curator cites Goya's painting *The Second of May*, depicting the Spanish resistance to Napoleon's invasion of Madrid, as an example of art as a sociopolitical statement. While that is important, it may not be sufficient, in the Curator's view, for "sometimes the spirit wears away / in the dust bowl of abuse." So art must do more than make a statement. It must impart a vision. Thus we move on, in Beta, to a notion of art as a paradoxical dialectic process, in which the wide view of the scientist can lead to mystery, while dreams may give rise to sharp insight.

But if one seeks the nth verisimilar
go to Ars by the way of Pisgah:
as the telescope of Galileo
deserted the clod to read the engirdling idioms of the star,
to the ape of God,
go!

In other words, if you are detail-oriented, take the long view to attain a global grasp of art.

> But if one, a lotus eater, seeks
>   the umbrella of the green bay tree,
>   go to Solomon's seal—
>   to the ant's synecdoche.[2]

The dreamer, on the other hand, the embracer of insubstantial visions, should study what is close at hand, see the ant as a representative of the larger world.

This canto also serves as an apologia for the Curator and his role in the poem. He believes he knows what is required to understand a work of art but fears he is not up to the task:

> "Great minds require of us a reading glass;
>   great souls a hearing aid."
>   But I,
>   in the shuttlebox world,
>   again and again,
>   have both mislaid.

He adds, disarmingly,

>   In the drama *Art*,
>   with eye and tongue
>   I play a minor vocative part,
>   like the O
>   of St. Bridget when it is rent
>   by the basso profundo
>   in the abysmal D
>   of his fortissimo
>   descent.[3]

He is, he says, merely an ex-professor of art. He has fraternized with the "Young Men labeled by their decades / The Lost, The Bright, The Angry, The Beat." But, he adds, "I was not gilded, like them, / with the gift of tongues. . . . / the upper rungs / of my ladder are zeros."

The next three cantos continue to elaborate the definition and purpose of art, as if to provide a defense of the artist's vocation. In Gamma's "babel city" where "sweating pilgrims" are jostled along "busybody roads," art may be submerged and lost. But we discover our extended selves, our otherness, in artifice:

> We who are we
> discover *altérité* in the actors on
> the boards of the Théâtre Vie.

Without art, "synapses of the thinking reed snap / from too little reality."

In Delta we learn that "The artist and his age . . . / are both aware / that God or Caesar is the handle / to the camel's hair." (That is, the sponsor who pays the bills wields the paintbrush.) What does it matter whether art is for art's sake or the church's or the world's? The ultimate purpose is still in question:

> Like the shape of Africa,
> the *raison d'être* of Art is a question mark:
> without the true flight of the bat,
> it is a hanker in the dark.
> Not as face answers face in water,
> but as windows answer each other . . .

Yet, says the Curator in Epsilon, people clamor for art to honor the heroes of the day. But in fact the classics have done that, and in so doing have transformed the local to the universal. The artist remains torn between God and Caesar, but he can go deeper, "under root and stone" to reveal "a whale's backbone."

So far we've been engaged in somewhat abstract discussions of the nature of art, its place in society, and its function in the psyche of the artist. All this is useful, but it's only a stage setting for the drama to come. If art is truly a human activity, we can understand it only as we see it created and responded to by people who mean something to us. It's time to bring characters onstage.

Canto Zeta introduces John Laugart, a half-blind painter and seer, "spoon-shaped like an aged parrot-fish . . . sighing / 'The eagle's wings / as well as the wren's, / grow weary of flying.'" Most of the canto is spent in describing the painter and his relation to the Curator in ever more baroque verbiage; but with a fuller picture comes a sense of his character and principles. Though partly drunk and in despair ("No man cares for my soul!"), Laugart insists that a work of art should be immortal and universal ("it does not lose its form and color / in native or in alien lands"), and he allows the artist no excuse for failure:

> "It matters not a tinker's dam
> on the hither or thither side of the Acheron[4]
> how many rivers you cross
> if you fail to cross the Rubicon!"

Laugart will prove one of the tragic figures in the poem; robbed and murdered in his flat and leaving behind a bottle of gin and "infamy / the Siamese twin / of fame."

With the Eta canto we come to one of the most substantial characters in the work, Dr. Obi Nkomo, "alter ego / of the Harlem Gallery." Like Laugart, he is committed without compromise to the artist's mission: "The lie of the artist is the only lie / for which a mortal or a god should die." His name and his residual tongue-click suggest he is from Africa, but he and the Curator are intellectual brothers with a nearly identical world view, though Nkomo is more assertive. He helps the Curator accession artwork.

> The therapy of his slips
> by design into primitive *objets d'art*
> humanized the patrons of the Harlem Gallery
> as much as the masterworks
> he salvaged from the Lethe
> of the American Way in Black Manhattan.

Challenged by one of the Gallery's philistine regents, Mr. Guy Delaporte III, Nkomo is unrepentant, for he has his own vision. "What is a masterpiece?" he asks,

> "A virgin or a jade,
> the *vis viva* of an ape of God,

> to awaken one,
>
> to pleasure one—
>
> a way-of-life's aubade."

Whether our measures are Greek (warning of the flaw of hubris) or Christian (deploring the sin of pride), there is no absolute standard of virtue, he maintains; therefore we cannot consider anyone beyond the pale.

Later, interrupted by some minor comic characters, Nkomo muses on man's thrall to sex. He relates a parable of an eagle found eating dung among chickens. Carried up a mountain (its proper domain) and launched into space, the eagle tumbles down again in disgrace. When a "giraffine man" at the bar asks Nkomo "Who are you?" the question leads to a long meditation: "*What* am I? *What* are you? / Perhaps we / are twin colors in a crystal." Asked again, in light of his parable, "*What* are you? / An eagle or a chicken come home to roost?" Nkomo demurs, "I wish I knew."

All this repartee serves to point to the twin hazards of soaring too high and falling too low, and the risk (a parallel theme throughout the poem) of caring too much about racial purity: There must be a middle path. "The golden mean / of the dark wayfarer's way between / black Scylla and white Charybdis, I / have traveled . . ." The true *Dies Irae,* maintains Nkomo (channeling Tolson), is spoken not by its composer, Thomas of Celano, but by Edward Gibbon, who chronicled the fall of the Roman empire as it strayed too far from the *via media.*

But having made that point, the poem proceeds, in Theta, to assert that the very opposites artists should avoid are inextricably blended in their best work:

> Something there is in Art that does not love a wall.
>
> Idea and image,
>
> form and content,
>
> blend like pigment with pigment
>
> in a flesh color.
>
> What dread hand can unmix
>
> pink and yellow?

Indeed, Tolson confesses his major operating principle throughout the poem—the juxtaposition of unlike things—when he states that "the miracle of the metaphor smites / disparate realms into a form / tighter than a mailed fist." In this way "Art . . . is a distant cousin of . . . Happiness." There is more to be said on this subject, and Tolson indeed says more. But for our limited purposes this much will suffice.

With Iota we come at last to "see" actual paintings, as the Harlem Gallery opens to admit guests to its new exhibition. Dr. Nkomo and the Curator are on hand to greet them. There are four wings in the gallery. The East Wing offers an atmosphere pervaded with "the nuances / of success and disaster." Its psychologically probing pictures, imbued with "broods of the ethos and artistic moods," present "[i]ronies and tensions of flesh / going to grass." The West Wing, combining modernist works with "blue/ tomtoms of Benin," appears to concentrate on portraits presented in theatrical fashion: upstage, downstage, and backstage. The North Wing has more portraits, but they seem to feature "every actor in the Harlem cast" while representing the human comedy "with *Bios* and *Societas* and *X* / as well as the divine." The South Wing offers a gallery of local heroes, a response to the sentiment of the patrons who cry: "We / have heroes! Celebrate *them* upon our walls!" Dr. Nkomo dubs this art dismissively "afterwit's aftermeat." But the Curator observes that even within elite artworks lurk ancient plebeian figures, the "voices of the voiceless," that give them vitality. These are, he says, "frescoes of bourgeois reality."

Kappa presents a comic interlude in which the philistine regent Mr. Guy Delaporte III, accompanied by his comely wife ("he, / with a frown like curd; / she, / with a smile like whey"), takes offense at John Laugart's "Black Bourgeoisie" for its failure to offer an exalted vision. There is, he complains, "No platinum black in the undifferentiated sand." To this Nkomo replies that the work of art "scatters its seeds quietly." And the Curator, likewise not directly challenging this influential and wealthy patron, calls attention to "the ghost of the thing / unsaid: / *Give voice to a bill / of faith at another hour.*" He cautions that there cannot be a sharp demarcation between one type of art and another. Invoking a rather far-fetched historical analogy, he notes that the failure of the Maginot Line to keep Germany from invading France did not stop Chagall, Matisse, and Picasso. All these conversations are attempts to determine whether art has boundaries of propriety or social acceptance—and whether there is an ideal audience to whom it should appeal.

That debate is propelled further in Lambda, when we encounter Hideho Heights, poet of the people and a major figure in the Harlem Gallery. In "a voice like a / ferry horn in a river of fog," he jokes with the Curator in the vernacular of the street and recites a poem in praise of Louis Armstrong "In the grand style / of a Doctor Faustus." The poem is not in the modernist style of Tolson's usual voice but in the manner of a popular ballad:

> *Where, oh, where is Bessie Smith*
> *with her heart as big as the blues of truth?*
> *Where, oh, where is Mister Jelly Roll*
> *with his Cadillac and diamond tooth?*
> *Where, oh, where is Papa Handy*
> *with his blue notes a-dragging from bar to bar?*
> *Where, oh, where is bulletproof Leadbelly*
> *with his tall tales and 12-string guitar?*

We will later see that Hideho Heights has two sides: a public "performance" manner and a private manner devoted to a higher and more esoteric form of art.

In Mu and Nu, Hideho and the Curator take in a performance of a jazz concert by Frog Legs Lux and the Indigo Combo, while observing and provoking some sexual byplay among the patrons, including the wits of the Zulu Club, who might be seen as Harlem's answer to the Algonquin Round Table. "Jazz is the marijuana of the Blacks," says Hideho. "Jazz is the philosophers' egg of the Whites," responds the Curator, implying that the uninitiated seek and study it as if it could provide a key to a deep and elusive mystery.[5] Provoked by an invitation from the MC and a plea from a "tipsy Lena / who peddled Edenic joys," Hideho condescends to recite another poem for the patrons.

In Xi, Hideho starts to perform his ballad "The Birth of John Henry." He is interrupted by Dipsy Muse and Wafer Waite, whose frenetic movements and comments reflect the high level of excitement in the room. Hideho is starting to show the effects of drink, and even the Curator breaks his cocktail glass. Despite or because of the tipsy atmosphere, the energy in the room is rapturous: "The creative impulse in the Zulu Club / leaps from Hideho's lips to Frog Legs' fingers / like the electric fire from the clouds." The Curator's one-time student Black Diamond takes the stage and rants. The Curator senses "thoughts springing clear of / the *terra firma* of the mind." This is art as possession, as ecstatic experience. But is it something to build on? Hideho sobs, "My *people*, / *my* people—/ they know not what they do."

In Omicron's more sober mood, Dr. Nkomo observes that life and art beget incestuously. That gnomic statement is interpreted to mean that each artist incorporates the work and thought of previous artists in his productions.

> Without Velazquez and Cranach
> what would Picasso be?
> Or Léger without Poussin?
> Or Amedeo Modigliani without Sandro Botticelli?

Interestingly, these questions all pertain to the history of painting. Tolson stays clear of the fraught questions of influence and inheritance in fiction and poetry. The rest of the canto offers aphorisms on art, and specifically on the nature and qualities of the artist. The aphorisms are aspirational; the artist is idealized throughout.

Pi offers a further lecture on the nature of art and the role of the critic, and here the ideas are more inventive. The voice behind the lecture is either Tolson's or the Curator's; they're often indistinguishable. The critic, we are told, must suppress his ego and point up details in the artwork. The lecture draws its examples from artists of the past, who are celebrated for invention, however unconventional, but not for destruction. The artist is adjured to transform the ordinary: "The harlot Now the master paints / aspires to hang in the gallery Hence / with Brueghel's knaves / and Cimabue's saints."

Rho introduces Mister Starks, the composer and "piano-modernist / of the Harlem Renaissance," and his wife Hedda, a "striptease has-been" who, it develops, has been a lover of Guy Delaporte III. We learn in this and the following canto that Starks has committed suicide, an "escape to the upper air." Nevertheless he seems very much present in the poem, and his contemplation of his achievements and failures forms a large part of *The Harlem Gallery's* atmosphere and effect.

Sigma continues the story, explaining that Starks, not yet dead, has sent a registered letter to a funeral home containing his last will and testament. Ma'am Shears, the owner, telephones Starks and tries to dissuade him from suicide. He blows her off, asserting that black people are civilized enough to kill themselves. Later Starks is discovered with a bullet in his heart, but the .38 is found in Crazy Cain's toilet bowl. When Hedda Starks ("Black Orchid") is arrested, she passes Starks's manuscript on to the Curator. We learn in Tau that the manuscript, "Harlem Vignettes," is a volume of imagistic verse. Its content forms the next canto.

In the fiction of *The Harlem Gallery,* the principal characters come together in Upsilon, in verse portraits, emulating paintings, composed by a musician. The series begins with a brutal self-assessment by Starks, who confesses, "My talent was an Uptown whore, my wit a Downtown pimp." Yet, in spite of a less than stellar career, he claims some renown for his *Black Orchid Suite.* He calls Hideho Heights "a crab louse / in the pubic region of Afroamerica," but quotes with approval his observation that "Content is a substance beneath the bark." His vignettes include character sketches of Dr. Igor Shears, a patron of the arts who "frequented deep water"; Crazy Cain, bastard son of Black Orchid and Guy Delaporte III, who was fired from the Harlem Symphony Orchestra by Starks and thus may have a motive for shooting him; Dr. Obi Nkomo, "a bastard of Barbarus and Cultura"; the Curator himself, as much akin to Nkomo as cream is to milk; and John Laugart, who is compared to Daumier: "the ominous rattle of his bones will never disturb / the tryst of graveyard lovers." This is art as social commentary in the manner of Balzac or Brueghel. Its aim is not impeccable accuracy but discovery of the telling and memorable detail.

Phi returns to the Curator's voice. He does not rate "Harlem Vignettes" highly but admits to being affected by it. Picking up the running theme of race, he observes that "plural strains mingle and run" through the concept of "the Negro" which "varies like a Siamese noun / with five different meanings in five different tones." After a debate between Kilroy (a minor character) and Nkomo, Hideho emerges and elaborately introduces his own poem, "The Sea Turtle and the Shark," a high point of Tolson's epic:

> Strange but true is the story
> of the sea-turtle and the shark—
> the instinctive drive of the weak to survive
> in the oceanic dark.
> Driven,
> riven
> by hunger
> from abyss to shoal,
> sometimes the shark swallows
> the sea-turtle whole.

The sly reptilian marine

withdraws,

into the shell

of his undersea craft,

his leathery head and the rapacious claws

that can rip

a rhinoceros' hide

or strip

a crocodile to fare-thee-well;

now,

inside the shark,

the sea-turtle begins the churning seesaws

of his descent into pelagic hell;

then . . . then,

with ravenous jaws

that can cut sheet steel scrap,

the sea-turtle gnaws

. . . and gnaws . . . and gnaws . . .

his way in a way that appalls—

his way to freedom,

beyond the vomiting dark,

beyond the stomach walls

of the shark.

The poem is, of course, a fable, and its meaning is clear. It is both aspirational and celebratory. It is more transparent than almost any other part of *The Harlem Gallery*, far removed from the dense, allusive, modernist style Tolson himself champions and employs. Despite the praise its hearers heap on it, it appears not to be the sort of poem on which Hideho Heights would like to pin his reputation.

And so, in Chi, we encounter the hermetic poem of Hideho's private life: *E. & O. E.*[6] This poem, liberally annotated in the manner of *The Waste Land*, is more squarely in the Eliotic tradition. It also happens to be the name of a poem written by Melvin Tolson, published by *Poetry* magazine, and the winner of its Bess Hokin award in 1952. Here Hideho's ambition confronts his achievement. Passages from *E. & O. E.* appear in his voice throughout this canto. His confession near the end could well be Tolson's own:

> I do not shake
> the Wailing Wall
> of Earth—
> nor quake
> the Gethsemane
> of Sea—
> nor tear
> the Big Top
> of Sky
> with Lear's prayer,
> or Barabas' curse,
> or Job's cry!

The penultimate canto, Psi, comprises a long meditation on race and art, focusing on the dilemma of the Black artist but aiming its instructions at both "Black Boy" and "White Boy." The author and the Curator merge to bring the canto to a not particularly hopeful conclusion:

> A Pelagian with the *raison d'être* of a Negro,
> I cannot say I have outwitted dread
> for I am conscious of the noiseless tread
> of the Yazoo tiger's ball-like pads behind me
> in the dark
> as I trudge ahead,
> up and up . . . that Lonesome Road . . . up and up.

Finally, Omega sums up the value of the gallery's collection, while encouraging the artist, white or black, to aspire:

> [T]his allegro of the Harlem Gallery
> is not a chippy fire,

> for here, in focus, are paintings that chronicle
> a people's New World odyssey
> from chattel to Esquire!

. . . .

What can we conclude from this difficult, multifaceted work? Part of its difficulty lies in its attempt to deal with both aesthetic and social issues at the same time. It is necessary to recognize, for example, that the question of the intended audience for an artwork may carry more weight in communities that have felt ignored or discouraged by long-established museums and concert halls. Consider the wide-eyed discovery by influential critics in our time of Black composers and painters of previous generations who were long omitted from the mainstream canons of their respective arts. Then you may understand the daunting distance Tolson's characters perceive between aspiration and achievement.

We can sum up the complex aesthetic discourse of the poem under three headings: *principles, practicalities, and precepts.* As a matter of principle, Tolson contends that art should make a statement. It should sharpen vision, and it should base its vision in reality. Its goal should be the search for a fundamental truth. It should be immortal (not time-bound) and universal (not place-bound). It should give pleasure; it should be "a distant cousin of happiness." It should fuse opposites and search for a mean.

In practical terms, artists need to recognize and accommodate both "high" and "low" art, and even a form of art that results in—or from—ecstatic possession. There must be venues, such as the Harlem Gallery, for many types of expression and the accompanying self-definition of artists and the societies they inhabit.

Those considerations lead to precepts, or injunctions laid upon the artists of a period and a community. Recognizing that art is a living thing that evolves over generations, they must be inventive and must transcend their own egos. They must dedicate themselves to producing an art rich and flexible enough to deal with their environment and the situation in which they find themselves, including the condition of being defined by the term "Negro."

But the Harlem Gallery is in no way a mere airing of grievances. It is an affectionate portrait of quirky, witty, and convincing characters in Harlem society, seen through their interactions and debates on serious matters of taste and judgment. It is a discussion of art in general and in many of its particulars. It is a multifaceted demonstration of poetic styles (and of its author's considerable erudition). Indeed—although I am not sure this is the quality I would praise most highly—it out-Eliots Eliot and out-Pounds Pound. It is and will remain a daunting book, but it deserves to be part of the tradition we pass on.

NOTES

1. Raymond Nelson, ed., *"Harlem Gallery" and Other Poems of Melvin B. Tolson* (University Press of Virginia, 1999). Nelson's notes clarify many obscure references and are an invaluable aid to readers. The introduction by Rita Dove provides useful context and an assessment of reactions by Tolson's contemporaries.

2. Solomon's seal is a plant, of course, but it is named for the Seal of Solomon, a signet ring with supposedly magical qualities.

3. There are various hymns to St. Bridget, but I have not so far found one with a descending bass line.

4. The river Acheron was the equivalent of the Styx.

5. One meaning of "philosophers' egg" is "philosophers' stone"—the long-sought substance capable of transmuting base metals to gold.

6. The letters are said to be a printers' term: Errors and Omissions Excepted.

11

ENTER AT YOUR OWN RISK
Poems of Vijay Seshadri

A certain animus runs through the work of a number of poets we esteem. Dryden's scorn for Thomas Shadwell begat "Mac Flecknoe." Pope turned figures in the court of George II, along with some literary rivals, into epitomes of dullness in "The Dunciad." Byron's competitive hostility toward Robert Southey is an animating force in "Don Juan." More recently Derek Walcott, in "The Mongoose," took a savage lick at V. S. Naipaul, a fellow Caribbean writer. Beyond personal vendettas, many poets have expressed hostility toward prevailing attitudes that they consider oppressive or insensitive. But rare is the poet who claims to be contemptuous not just of a rival or a pernicious trend, but of readers in general. Though Robert Frost famously said he had "a lover's quarrel with the world," that world seemed always more distant and impersonal than the admirers who eagerly read his poems. So it is unusual, to say the least, to encounter a writer deeply suspicious of his readers and evidently intent on avoiding them. Is such an attitude sincere, or is it a fiction with an artful motive?

If you wanted—if you believed you were entitled—to adopt an air of jaded wisdom, you could say (if you were in fact tired of the imagination's long-running charade) that we've seen it all before, in poems stretching back over centuries. We've seen allegory, detachment, revelation, self-revelation, communion with nature, confession, celebration, and complaint. We've seen ideas about the thing and we've seen the thing itself (or so it's said). And yet we're suspicious and discouraged. We're anxious and troubled and disillusioned. Who can possibly speak to us in our frayed condition? Anybody? Maybe only someone who doesn't trust us any more than we trust him. Someone who

158

hears the Angel of Death in the guise of a little girl say "Beauty and sadness are never far apart" and responds "Bullshit." Who hears her say "Some birds are real, some are invisible, but which are which?" and growls "Back off, bitch" ("Your Living Eyes").[1]

In short, someone who's not seduced by his own imagination and is not out to seduce us. Or even to have much to do with us. Someone who begrudges the merest encounter:

I'll meet you if you really want to meet.
I'll even meet you in some small café or some
park across the way. But I won't meet for long,
and not for a minute will I look at you in your isolation . . .

—"Meeting (Thick)"[2]

So who is this guy? Well you might ask. "Who Is This Guy?" is the title of one of the poems in this collection, and one of the more transparent ones at that. In it, the author sees himself as the dead remnant of a once-living self. Safely killed, he can tempt the still-living (and himself) with the seductive tokens of a remembered vitality. But, he asserts, he can withstand the temptation himself because he's safely dead. The dead, it seems, are those who, cut off from the maelstrom of sensation (such isolation being a necessary shield for a writer, some would argue), are yet able to use elements of it to awaken the still-living. Who is this guy, then? You might say he's a partially anesthetized, sober-voiced reincarnation of Hilda Doolittle, who cried (in "Orchard") "spare us from loveliness." And in his own poem he evokes suspiciously lovely details like "that summer night. / The long shadows. The risen full moon / [that] casts a veil of leaf shadows over a face," only to shudder:

The longing is as if it were a knife, and for that longing alone—
piercing and inevitable—
the living, the beautiful living, would, if I weren't already dead,
kill me again and again.

Are you beginning to see the program? Seshadri is neither cynical nor insensitive to the beguiling wonders around him. He is as susceptible as anyone else to natural beauty, human warmth, and the unanswerable losses we all must face. In fact he is in constant danger of being overwhelmed and destroyed. So he erects barriers. He will not be demonstrative. He will avoid display. His defense is irony.

As he says in his opening poem, he has tried to communicate directly, but "I'm sick of being slaughtered in my life's mountain passes, / covering my own retreat, / the rear guard of my own brutal defeat." And so "I'm just going to drive away down the coast / and not come back" ("Road Trip"). If he has special knowledge or perceptions, he'll take them with him rather than share them with others: "The secrets I was planning to floor them with? / They're already packed in my trunk, in straw." Henceforward his wisdom, such as it is, will no longer be spoken in his own voice. "I'll scatter those truths to the sea breezes / . . . and then I'll just be there, in the sunset's coppery sheen. . . . Look at the clouds. Look how close they are." It may be a little hopeful, but that's his program. You can take it or leave it.

I'm spending time elucidating this poet's attitudes because the poems are difficult and often complex. They speak through many fictive voices, and most of the voices are heavy with irony. It should be clear by now that Seshadri is not out to make friends with us. His book is a constructed thicket of thorns with a sign posted that says Enter at Your Own Risk. Some readers experience a certain frisson in venturing into hostile territory, just as some adventurers experience a surge of triumph in scaling K2 in winter without supplemental oxygen. A poet (who despite apparent insouciance is less indifferent than a mountain) relies on their intrepidity. All right, then, reader. Once you've reached the top, what do you find?

Let's start with the physical layout. The poems tend to be written in long, unmetered lines that break off whenever the poet chooses. They're long enough that the book designer decided to make the book extra wide to accommodate them. The poem called "Meeting" in its "thick" and "thin" versions was evidently an experiment by the author: which version might work best? He couldn't decide, apparently, so he included both. (I prefer the "thin" version because it slows the reader down, but most of the other poems use longer lines that must seem more congenial to Seshadri.)

There's little regular rhyme, except in the poem called "Nemesis," but there are many instances of what we might call casual rhyme that crops up here and there like the smile of the Cheshire cat:

The black wine is aerating.
The pasta is limp and waiting
to be sauced and tossed.
There is a clue to find.
There is an innocence
to establish and an anguish in
him he needs to destroy
before it destroys him, an
anguish so pure it almost
feels like joy.

    —"City of Grief"

Because rhyme and meter are captivating, a way of bringing readers into line and enlisting their sympathies on a visceral level, it's understandable that Seshadri avoids these devices most of the time. He's not out to make the reader a friend or an ally. He poses as one who doesn't expect to be liked, though I'm not altogether convinced by the pose. He's capable of evocative descriptive language ("obsidian tide pools that cradle the ribbed limpet," "goshawks rising on their thermals," the latter observed as he contemplates falling from a plane without a parachute), though he keeps such flourishes severely in check. He indulges an odd verbal tic, in which an assertion is made, then repeated at once with an intensifier: "I am. I guess I am." "Yes, it is, it really is." "I would, I know, I surely would."[3] But mainly the language is challenging, tough, as if to say "You wanna make something of it?":

You keep complaining that there are two people inside me—

The one confident, decisive, ironic;
the other a raging cripple
who never took to the nipple,
whose life has been one long
episode of colic.
Just admit you don't know which one you like better,
which one rings your bell.
I happen to like them both.

    —"Marriage"

You can see from these examples, and indeed from most of the poems in this book, that the author is focused intensely on himself—his stance in relation to the world, the way he is perceived. It's a position continually under negotiation, on his side at least.

Behind every poem, by any poet, lies a choice its author has made, consciously or not, about how to communicate with the reader. The options are myriad: in the poet's own voice or in an assumed objective tone; ironically or with evident sincerity; as a friend, an advisor, a plaintiff, or one aggrieved. You, the reader, are placed under a corresponding obligation to discern or intuit the author's intent. But first—are you engaged? Intrigued? Seduced? Repelled? Willing to follow despite complexities? Will you join the dance? Your decision may depend on your finding a way in: a poem or passage that will compel you to read further, to follow the writer into his own territory, where, you hope, something important will be revealed.

Surveying this varied, multifaceted book, I find it hard to single out one poem as a masterpiece, a beautifully achieved object. But beautiful achievements are not what the poems are about. They're documents in the writer's struggle with himself and with the world around him. That in itself may be worth our attention. To get a closer look at the nature of that struggle, and the stakes involved, consider "Cliffhanging," a poem dedicated to a dead friend, the poet Tom Lux, whom Seshadri obviously admired. It begins:

> The forces out to kill us with their benevolence
> are more crazed now than they were when you were alive.
> And more focused too. Our ingratitude excites them.
> They're bubbling with remedies.
> Their providential impulses are a nimbus of knives.
> Their need to tell us they love us, love us,
> with all their love in vain . . .

These are the meliorists with easy answers and too-quick sympathy, against whom one must be on guard. The poet goes on to address his dead friend: "You said before you died that this would happen. / Thanks for the warning." But, he adds, he didn't realize that even the perceptions recorded in their poems ("our phantom selves") would come after them, "crawling out of the poems we made." These heightened sensibilities, zombie-like, "see more than they can stand," things "we could never really bear to see"—and as such they threaten to destroy the pair. "They've cut the phone lines, / and are chain-sawing the front door."

With a certain bravado, he confesses that "all this hostility from every quarter bothers me / much less than it should." He feels himself lifted by a great wave, dragged inland, then dropped on a cliff's edge, hanging on by one arm. "I won't let myself fall, but I don't want to pull myself up." So is his friend in a kind of paradise, outside this world, or is he someone who's made his peace with things as they are? The readiest interpretation is that he's offering to pull the author into the land of the dead—an offer the latter is inclined to accept (though he's ambivalent, for that land is unlikely to be a paradise). Whatever it is or isn't, the implication is that it's preferable to present reality:

> But if you were here, looking down on me and saying,
> "Grab my hand, grab my hand," I would, I know, I surely would.

Would he like to be with his friend, or would he like to be dead? Or both?

"Cliffhanging," rife as it is with ambiguity, is one of the more successful of the poems. The author asserts that he doesn't want to feel what he has felt, perceive what he has perceived. While he claims not to be unduly troubled, he also states that he's overwhelmed and almost ready to give up. A poem like this recalls us to the land, and the state of mind, of Robert Lowell, who cried out (in "Skunk Hour," echoing Milton's Satan), "I myself am hell; / nobody's here—" except that Seshadri filters his undoubtedly genuine disquiet through layers of irony and self-scrutiny that keep readers in constant doubt as to just what is sincere interior turmoil and what is performance.

The problem with that stance, maintained with some variations throughout the entire book, is that it threatens to become a shtick. Does hostility truly come at him from every quarter, as he claims, and if so, what is its source and its nature? How, in the world of the poem to which we're granted access, can we distinguish paranoia from rationality? Where should our sympathies lie? Is the poet drowning or just waving?

Somewhere behind the postures and protestations is a remarkably acute and reactive sensibility who feels himself, as he says in "Soliloquy," coming face to face with horror. He hastens to qualify that statement: it is "the moment before the last," which, he believes, "stretches across eternity." This is a particular kind of horror that Seshadri is not the first to observe. A century ago Paul Valéry complained:

> Zeno, O cruel Zeno of Elea!
> You've pierced my center with your feathered lance
> That vibrates, flies, and never can advance.[4]

We are caught forever in the moment just before the end. It's a perception we often manage to ignore—except when we cannot.[5]

I will not return often to this book for its beautiful phrases or its wisdom or even its flashes of insight—though insight is not lacking here. I may go back on occasion to reacquaint myself with a record of the anguish felt by a perceptive man who feels nearly overwhelmed by his world. But I will remain frustrated by the record's failure to explain just what were the forces arrayed against the sufferer. I expect I will be alternately entertained and annoyed by the feints and disguises laid out to obscure the writer's position. I will wish, and I'm sure the author wishes, for more revelation than is granted by a fortune cookie picked up at the Milwaukee airport: "Life cries out *Be*." But that's all he wrote.

Or almost all—except for an envoi addressed "To the Reader" in which the poet asserts that "what you're thinking / about me is exactly what I'm thinking / about you." He undercuts that statement by claiming that all these words (both the writer's and the reader's) "have no meaning, / only form." It's one more barrier, mask, disguise, this time in the form of a mirror. Like similar devices scattered through the book, it's an unneeded disavowal.

NOTES

This chapter originated as a review of Vijay Seshadri's book "That Was Now, This Is Then" (Graywolf Press, 2020).

1. The words quoted do not purport to be the poet's but those of his father. But they're endorsed and, in effect, seconded by the poet, as the poem's last lines make clear. As for the sentiments so rudely refuted, the first will be found in Keats's "Ode on Melancholy," the second in Stevens's "Thirteen Ways of Looking at a Blackbird."

2. There are two versions of this poem. The other (immediately following) is "Meeting (Thin)," which contains roughly twice as many lines, each of roughly half the length. The versions are identical in content except that "uninflected" in the first poem is replaced by "thin" in the second.

3. From, respectively, "Commas, Dashes, Ellipses, Full Stops, Question Marks," "Collins Ferry Landing," and "Cliffhanging."

4. From "The Graveyard by the Sea," my translation.

5. A not-irrelevant tangent: in "Man and Woman Talking," a dramatic dialogue in part 3 of this book, after a married couple's exchange of mutual hostility and misunderstanding, the husband "walks across the stage while reading" Henry Vaughan's poem "I saw Eternity the other night," implying that he too is trapped in that endless penultimate moment.

IV. THE WAY FORWARD

12

FORMALISTS AGAINST THE TIDE
What They Learned from the Tide

The English-speaking peoples have always felt that the difference between poetic speech and the conversational speech of everyday should be kept small,
and, whenever English poets have felt that the gap between poetic and ordinary
speech was growing too wide, there has been a stylistic revolution to bring them
closer again.

—W. H. Auden, *The Dyer's Hand*

Formal poetry, like the acoustic guitar, is now tagged with an adjective that
marks its consignment to a corner of the realm it once ruled. Poets writing
mainly in form today are considered—if not conservative—at least conservators of a venerable tradition of craft, one that for a while in the previous century was threatened with extinction. They are thought to have turned inward,
away from the daring (or liberating) free-verse experiments of their contemporaries, to practice a hermetic kind of artistry almost quaint in its obsession
with stress and syllable counts, its concern with caesuras and enjambment.
By contrast, the apostles of the new were convinced in their heyday that "the
strongest and most alive poetry in America had abandoned or at least broken
the grip of traditional meters."[1]

I want to suggest that something more complex was going on. Old ways
of writing were indeed being revitalized, and much was made by the revolu-
tionaries—especially the generation following William Carlos Williams—of
their freedom from the constraints of artifice. But the twentieth century was
in fact a vast laboratory in which poets of all dispositions worked to reconceive

their language and their approach to composition. Those who continued to write in meter and to employ rhyme made gains at least as noteworthy as their ostensibly liberated colleagues. To see why even an apparently conservative choice marked a distinct advance in poetic practice, we need to look back at the currents and storms of the early twentieth century.

For the moment, consider merely style and diction. Here are two examples to contemplate:

When that was, the soft mist
Of my regret hung not on all the land,
And I was glad for thee,
And glad for me, I wist.

Thou didst not know, who tottered, wandering on high,
That fate had made thee for the pleasure of the wind,
With those great careless wings,
Nor yet did I.

　　—Robert Frost, "My Butterfly," first published in 1894

'Twas not until the gods had been
Kindly entreated, and been brought within
Unto the hearth of their heart's home
That they might do this wonder thing;
Nathless I have been a tree amid the wood
And many a new thing understood
That was rank folly to my head before.

　　—Ezra Pound, "The Tree," before 1908

Far removed as these examples are from the patterns of spoken English current in the late nineteenth and early twentieth centuries, when the poems were written, they were very much in the poetic mainstream of their time—that is, the writings of Swinburne, the Rossettis, and the other pre-Raphaelite descendants who dominated English verse and who worked in a tradition dating back to Edmund Spenser, one that sanctioned the use of deliberately archaic diction as a way of suggesting an elevated tone and sensibility.

But although such diction was prevalent, it was by no means the only option available. Thomas Hardy and even William Butler Yeats were writing in a far more idiomatic style at the same time Frost and Pound were producing these poems—as was Edwin Arlington Robinson on American shores. Nevertheless, it was easy for a young poet to fall into the traditional style strongly associated with the poetry of status. And, because that style was usually couched in iambic meters and presented in ingenious stanzaic patterns involving complex rhyme schemes, some of the most influential writers concluded that in order to revitalize poetry the whole apparatus would have to be jettisoned and a new start made.

In *Missing Measures*, Timothy Steele observes that Eliot, in his critical writing, conflated idiom with metric. Referencing Wordsworth's attempt at the start of the nineteenth century to reform the language of poetry, Eliot extrapolates: "By the beginning of the present [twentieth] century another revolution in idiom—and such revolutions bring with them an alteration of metric, a new appeal to the ear—was due."[2] Perhaps because poets of the Victorian period had employed a pompous, sonorous, and stilted declamatory style when reading aloud (a style not altogether unknown even in mid-twentieth-century America), meter was blamed by many for the fustian quality of traditional poetry and was accordingly condemned.

And not just meter. Rhyme was denounced as well, for two reasons. First, it was considered a symptom of contrivance, an indicator that the writer was not setting down his impressions in an honest and straightforward manner but was out to trick and seduce the reader by adorning his sentences with verbal flourishes. And second, the rebels maintained that rhyme forced poets to distort their sentences by wrenching their grammar about to position like-sounding words properly and by introducing tangential notions into their discourse merely for verbal harmony. Even if a poet was successful in rhyming without violence to his sentences, he would not likely get credit for sincerity. He must free himself to be credible. "When the comforting echo of rhyme is removed," Eliot counseled, "success or failure in the choice of words, in the sentence structure, in the order, is at once more apparent. Rhyme removed, the poet is at once held up to the standards of prose."[3]

So on the one hand, verse ought to become more like prose. On the other hand, according to some writers, it should aspire to the condition of music. The goal was, as William Carlos Williams expressed it, "A [musical] bar, definitely, since it is not related to grammar, but to time. . . . The clause, the sentence

. . . are ignored, and the progression goes over into the next bar as much as the musical necessity requires . . . a sequence of musical bars arranged vertically on the page, and capable of infinite modulation."[4] Of course an actual musical bar contains a fixed number of beats, not unlike an iambic line—but what Williams probably had in mind was a musical phrase, which, not being of fixed length, can indeed span bar lines and is determined at least in part by the composer's intentions. But that is not a true prosody. It is a license for the poet to say, "The line is whatever I want it to be." In practice the verbal equivalent of a musical phrase was often a syntactic phrase.

The problem was compounded by a belief that meter was simply a matter of style, one associated with the language of a particular place and time and therefore capable of wholesale revision or replacement in light of new conditions. In an influential article, Williams asserted, "English prosody is not, finally, an inevitable deterministic dispensation from the gods; it is an historical development growing from English conditions—moral and historical which constitute her history."[5] Linguistically naïve as it was, this belief gave Williams and his compatriots license to jettison meter as a contrivance of the old world, inapplicable to American needs; it also allowed English poets, insofar as they accepted it, to conclude that a device suited to the "historical" conditions of their fathers was of no further use to them.

Behind these observations and gropings lay a pervasive dissatisfaction with the condition of poetry as these writers found it, together with an envy of art forms that seemed, from the outside at least, more authentic, less cumbered by artifice, more capable of fostering in the auditor a strong emotional response to keenly perceived experience. Different as the proponents were, they agreed on the need to remake poetry, something that could be done only by the generation now rising, and by those who needed poetry and cherished a devotion to its possibilities. But they were indeed a diverse group. They included Englishmen like T. E. Hulme and Ford Madox Hueffer (later Ford), who rebelled against what they saw as the hidebound pomposity of their elders; opportunistic Americans like Ezra Pound, whose mind was filled partly with the diction of Swinburne, partly with that of Browning, and partly with a fancied American backcountry twang that he never tired of burlesquing—an inspired parodist who, I would argue, never found his own voice; others like T. S. Eliot, conservative by nature and radical by association, who reinvented himself to fit the setting he aspired to; and lone wolves like Robert Frost and Wallace Stevens, averse to manifestoes, movements, and programs, who came to grips with reality and their moment in history in vastly different ways.

In short, within the small circle of serious poets working at the start of the twentieth century, one could find a wide array of attitudes and dispositions, even allowing for a general agreement that poetry had to change. We might range them on a scale from Classic to Romantic, or we might politicize the poles as Conservative and Radical, or we might dignify them with the terms Apollonian and Dionysian. Regardless, there were those who wished to throw out all vestiges of the old ways of writing, and others who either had a fondness for traditional techniques or could not altogether eradicate the habits they had grown up with. Among the former, Williams himself was one of the most effective writers (at least some of the time) and, in his later years, one of the most influential. His best verse did indeed have the virtues of good prose: it was clean, sharply perceived, and in some contexts capable of a certain eloquence.

> All along the road the reddish
> purplish, forked, upstanding, twiggy
> stuff of bushes and small trees
> with dead, brown leaves under them
> leafless vines—
>
> Lifeless in appearance, sluggish
> dazed spring approaches—
>
> They enter the new world naked,
> cold, uncertain of all
> save that they enter. All about them
> the cold, familiar wind—
>
> —"By the Road to the Contagious Hospital," from *Spring and All*

(Note that the last six lines, when read aloud, turn easily into four lines of respectable iambic pentameter.)

Because he championed a kind of back-to-the-earth romanticism, with an emphasis on observed detail rather than intellection ("No ideas but in things"),

Williams became a strong influence on a later generation of American writers distrustful of abstract thought and formal discipline. That generation included the popular phenomenon Allen Ginsberg and the incoherent but influential Charles Olson.[6] Many saw Williams as democratizing poetry. As James Dickey noted, he "appealed to many aspiring writers who looked at his work and said, 'Well if that's poetry, I believe I might be able to write it too!'"[7]

At the other end of the scale, Robert Frost embraced formal discipline. He continued writing metered poems, very often rhymed, even while modernizing his language and managing to fit idiomatic expressions into the confines of a predetermined structure, as in "A Girl's Garden":

> A neighbor of mine in the village
>   Likes to tell how one spring
> When she was a girl on the farm, she did
>   A childish thing.
>
> One day she asked her father
>   To give her a garden plot
> To plant and tend and reap herself,
>   And he said, "Why not?"

The lines in this case are loose iambics (three, three, four, and two stresses per line) with frequent anapestic substitutions that produce a fair imitation of speech while remaining recognizably verse.

For a while these were more or less the extremes. But there was a wide middle ground in which writers experimented with various compromise positions. Marianne Moore produced elaborately patterned syllabic verse that was considered experimental because it rejected traditional meter but was nevertheless often as highly stylized as any of Swinburne's creations. That it could not be registered by the ear as rhythm was partly mitigated by her strategic deployment of rhyme and by the ingenuity of concepts and choice of image invigorating her poems.

Whatever his critical pronouncements, T. S. Eliot managed to straddle the stylistic divide. He was, at times, capable of setting down naturalistic detail in elegant free verse:

The river's tent is broken; the last fingers of leaf
Clutch and sink into the wet bank. The wind
Crosses the brown land, unheard. The nymphs are departed.

    —"The Waste Land," III

And he could shift fluidly into a rhymed iambic meter with a rather sardonic tone:

She turns and looks a moment in the glass,
Hardly aware of her departed lover;
Her brain allows one half-formed thought to pass:
"Well now that's done; and I'm glad it's over."

    —"The Waste Land," III

For this facility, and for other qualities, he was prized by readers eager to find value in modern verse and willing to work for it; at the same time, he was roundly scorned by the more radically inclined, who felt he was betraying the revolution. But no one could argue that he had not modernized the language of poetry. From his earliest mature work Eliot had written a convincing idiom not only free of archaisms but reflecting, in generally iambic measures, the vistas and the demotic speech of his adopted city, London:

Shall I say, I have gone at dusk through narrow streets
And watched the smoke that rises from the pipes
Of lonely men in shirt-sleeves, leaning out of windows? . . .

    —"Prufrock"

You are a proper fool, I said,
Well, if Albert won't leave you alone, there it is, I said,
What you get married for if you don't want children?

    —"The Waste Land," II

The other major poet of the period who managed to present himself at once as a thoroughgoing modernist and a guardian of tradition was Wallace Stevens. He wrote idiomatic free verse studded with unexpected detail:

> People are not going
> To dream of baboons and periwinkles.
> Only, here and there, an old sailor,
> Drunk and asleep in his boots,
> Catches tigers
> In red weather.
>
> —"Disillusionment of Ten O'Clock"

He peppered his lines with strange, exuberant sound effects. At the same time, he was capable of writing, in "Sunday Morning," what Robert B. Shaw has called "one of the great blank-verse poems not just of the twentieth century but of all time."[8] The diction of "Sunday Morning," while complex at points, is graceful and unstrained. It is at once contemporary and elevated in idiom, except when Stevens deliberately imitates—but only for a moment—the quasi-biblical language of a faith the poem is explicitly renouncing:

> There is not any haunt of prophecy,
> Nor any old chimera of the grave,
> Neither the golden underground, nor isle
> Melodious, where spirits gat them home,
> Nor visionary south, nor cloudy palm
> Remote on heaven's hill, that has endured
> As April's green endures; or will endure
> Like her remembrance of awakened birds,
> Or her desire for June and evening, tipped
> By the consummation of the swallow's wings.

Modernist though he was, in language and in prosodic techniques (I use the plural advisedly), Stevens evidently harbored some nostalgia for a formality of language and style that he had imbibed in youth but that was now out of reach. He pays it affectionate tribute in "Mozart, 1935," where he adjures the poet to be seated at the piano and

Play the present, its hoo-hoo-hoo,
Its shoo-shoo-shoo, its ric-a-nic,
Its envious cachinnation.

But if that is music for a contemporary audience, he distrusts the audience:

If they throw stones upon the roof
While you practice arpeggios,
It is because they carry down the stairs
A body in rags.

In short, the remains of the old poetry. The heedless champions of newness
are, we may infer, thugs. But to the figure of the poet Stevens defiantly invokes
the language of Shelley as he calls for a new voice for the times:

Be thou the voice,
Not you, Be thou, be thou
The voice of angry fear,
The voice of this besieging pain.

Be thou that wintery sound
As of the great wind howling
. . .

Mozart, says Stevens, was young, and we are old. Life is uncontrolled:
"the streets are full of cries. / Be seated, thou." The language of that bygone
generation is no longer ours, but it can still be recalled, if only in fantasy, by
the century's greatest modernist to speak the age's anxieties through the for-
malities of art, grace, and discipline that serve as a bulwark against anarchy.

Stevens died in 1955, two years before Jack Kerouac published *On the Road*.
Frost's death in 1963 coincided with the rise of the youth culture in both
England and America, a culture that gave new energy to Romantic values
privileging impulse, feeling, and unfettered sexuality over reason, analysis,
and restraint. Poets who subscribed to an aesthetic in line with those values
found themselves well received by the young. Editors of journals soon adopted
policies favoring free verse and often explicitly proscribing anything written

in meter or rhyme. Allen Ginsberg, once considered a poet of the California fringe, was reverently received at the convention of the Modern Language Association, where he was invited to address the rapt assembled English professors, many of them recent converts to the cause.

In 1969 Stephen Berg and Robert Mezey published *Naked Poetry,* an anthology of recent American poetry in "open forms," which they defined as poems that "don't rhyme (usually) and don't move on feet of more or less equal duration (usually)."[9] The anthology conferred status and a wider readership on such poets as Weldon Keyes, W. S. Merwin, William Stafford, and Philip Levine, while revalidating the already established reputations of Theodore Roethke, John Berryman, and Allen Ginsberg. But the traditionalists did not fold. A few years later, X. J. Kennedy, one of the poets born in the 1920s who still favored metrical verse, often rhymed, joined his wife in launching a journal called *Counter/Measures,* whose express mission was to provide an outlet for writers working in form who found their publishing opportunities narrowing with the shift in editorial preference.

In response to the preeminence of free verse, many poets who preferred formally structured poems or in fact needed a metrical frame on which to construct an argument began exploring alternative approaches. Some embraced the syllabic meters that had been employed early in the century by Marianne Moore in America and by Elizabeth Daryush, her exact contemporary, in England. Difficult for auditors to hear (seven-syllable lines, the most common kind, are often perceived as loose three- or four-foot iambic lines), syllabics have the virtue of forcing careful word choice on the poet and freeing her from verbal formulas associated with iambic meters. Other poets discovered an interest in half-rhymes, in which either vowel sounds or consonant clusters (usually the latter), but not both, were matched, to produce a muted but clearly audible effect. This again was not a new technique, having been used extensively by Emily Dickinson a hundred years previously in poems not widely known until the age of modernism:

> The difference between Despair
> And Fear—is like the One
> Between the instant of a Wreck—
> And when the Wreck has been—

The Mind is smooth—no Motion—
Contented as the Eye
Upon the Forehead of a Bust—
That knows—it cannot see—

    —Collected Poems, 305

In the hands of some twentieth-century poets it was a mode to be employed occasionally, not constantly, when seeking a less insistent harmony:

The puzzled pilgrims come, car after car,
With cameras loaded for epiphanies;
For views of failure to take home and prize,
The dying tourists ride through realms of fire.

    —Howard Nemerov, "For Robert Frost, in the Autumn, in Vermont"

But for others it became a predominant mode, given a boost when Robert Pinsky used it throughout his translation of Dante's *Inferno* as a form of *terza rima* that required fewer awkward compromises for the sake of rhyme.

In one way the abandonment of regular meter made some of the free-verse partisans less adventurous than they might have been. Williams's concept of the "variable foot," while never clearly articulated, was interpreted by many followers to refer to a phrasal unit that could determine a line of verse. In other words, a line was often seen as a unit of speech terminated by a pause, which in practice was usually a punctuation mark. The result, in some poems, was a set of lines each of which was also a self-contained grammatical phrase. Here, for example, is the opening of Roethke's "The Far Field":

I dream of journeys repeatedly:
Of flying like a bat deep into a narrowing tunnel,
Of driving alone, without luggage, out a long peninsula,
The road lined with snow-laden second growth,
A fine snow ticking the windshield,
Alternate snow and sleet, no on-coming traffic,
And no lights behind, in the blurred side-mirror,

> The road changing from glazed tarface to a rubble of stone,
> Ending at last in a hopeless sand-rut,
> Where the car stalls,
> Churning in a snowdrift
> Until the headlights darken.

By contrast, poets who accepted the principle of an independent meter, determined by its own rules for the counting of stresses and syllables, were able to stretch syntax across line-endings, providing a perceptible contrast between the structure of the sentence and the structure of the verse. Here is Roethke's older contemporary Louise Bogan in "Old Countryside":

> Long since, we pulled brown oak-leaves to the ground
> In a winter of dry trees; we heard the cock
> Shout its unplaceable cry, the axe's sound
> Delay a moment after the axe's stroke.
>
> Far back, we saw, in the stillest of the year,
> The scrawled vine shudder, and the rose-branch show
> Red to the thorns, and, sharp as sight can bear,
> The thin hound's body arched against the snow.

Not all the lines without punctuation at the end are true enjambments; there is an implied syntactic pause, for example, at the end of the first line. But the next two lines clearly spill over to the following lines, as does the second line in the next stanza, and this tension between grammar and pacing, reinforced by rhyme, gives the poem an energy of movement that contributes to its propulsive effect.

Of course, some free-verse poets, especially in later years, had no compunctions about breaking a line across syntax—in some cases the more radically the better—to produce a more-or-less arbitrary lineation, as in Frank O'Hara's well-known "The Day Lady Died":

> I walk up the muggy street beginning to sun
> and have a hamburger and a malted and buy
> an ugly New World Writing to see what the poets
> in Ghana are doing these days

A case might be made that the first three lines contain five stresses apiece and thus exhibit what Annie Finch calls the ghost of meter,[10] but there might just as well be three or six stresses per line, depending on how one chooses to count, so it's not a strong enough ghost to pit against the poem's syntax. Where there is neither a metrical undercurrent nor a sequence of self-contained phrases to organize the discourse, there can be no question of a counterpoint between them. We are left with the words alone, and what the words convey. In brief, we have prose.

· · · ·

Later generations of poets, those who began writing in the forties or after, were thus in a position to profit by some of the gains made on both sides of the aisle. The first gain, as we have seen, was in diction. The language of the poetry being written as they matured was far more like colloquial speech than it had been thirty years earlier. At times it could loosen meter beyond recognition and instead use repetition and internal rhyme as structuring devices, as when W. D. Snodgrass writes:

> Whatever you've learned from each other
> must be turned from, turned against—
> against each other in the new curriculum.
> Whose pillowtalk, now, will substantiate the day done,
> the day that's still to do?
>
> —"A Separation Anthem"

But it could also, and oftener, present itself in graceful idiomatic phrases strung across the iambic line, as when Elizabeth Bishop writes:

> Look down into the courtyard. All the houses
> are built that way, with ornamental urns
> set on the mansard roof-tops where the pigeons
> take their walks.
>
> —"Paris, 7 A.M."

Thus the second gain was really a retention: the ability to play syntax and phrasing against a regular meter—something lost to writers of free verse.

Third, twentieth-century poetics expanded the range of rhymes, adding half-rhyme as a structural element, not just a variant or a supplement like an internal rhyme or consonance. As readers grew more used to hearing half-rhymes, poets worked with them more frequently. Many considered them a subtler form of sound-matching, noticeable but not insistent. Their use undeniably enlarged the resources of poets facing the inevitable need to rhyme on "love" and "death."

Fourth, poets who stayed with meter widened the applications of blank verse. As Shaw notes, "The extraordinary rise of the short lyric or epigrammatic poem in blank verse is one of the most significant legacies of the century."[11] And in the hands of writers like David Mason the blank-verse novel has gained (or maintained) a respectable if modest audience. In addition, poets learned, with some success, to write shorter unrhymed measures with an iambic pulse, as Nemerov did in "The Mud Turtle":

> He rests an hour in the garden,
> His alien presence observed by all:
> His lordly darkness decked in filth
> Bearded with weed like a lady's favor . . .

Others made a practice of syllabics, the standard meter of French verse but one that remained, for the most part, under the radar in the English-speaking world because listeners register stress above syllable count whether or not the stress occurs in regular patterns.

Finally, and most obviously, poets inclined to write metrically learned the advantages of abandoning meter on occasion. Sometimes the result seemed deceptively prose-like, as in Robert Lowell's poem "Returning":

> Nothing is deader than this small town main street,
> where the venerable elm sickens, and hardens
> with tarred cement, where no leaf
> is born, or falls, or resists till winter.

And sometimes the ghost of meter hung in the air, ready to vanish as soon as one sought it, but imparting still a sense of order, set off by touches of rhyme:

Leave him alone for a moment or two,
and you'll see him with his head
bent down, brooding, brooding,
eyes fixed on some chip,
some stone, some common plant,
the commonest thing,
as if it were the clue.
The disturbed eyes rise,
furtive, foiled, dissatisfied
from meditation on the true
and insignificant.

    —Lowell, "Hawthorne"

Wide-ranging options for writing verse do not of course ensure that excellent poetry will be written, but they do make it possible. The task of any poet, faced with a bombardment of sensory impression, a vast reservoir of recollected experience and images, and the disorderly swirl of feeling that accompanies them, is to select, record, and respond. Poets do so with the means granted not just by their native abilities but also by their moment in history, their relation to language, and their place in the world. With such means, great or small, poets must, in Bishop's words, spar with the sun.

It is clear that the possibilities available by midcentury to poets of all stripes were far greater than the ones prevailing when Frost and Pound were apprentices. The wider resources were the result of numerous experiments, battles, mistakes, and a few remarkable successes in the first decades of the century. In the nineteen-sixties and seventies it seemed that the struggle between metered and unmetered verse had been all but decided in favor of the latter. But not everyone was convinced. There was still an audience for measure, and there were still writers committed to it. After Bishop and Lowell came the likes of Brooks, Hecht, Nemerov, Justice, Snodgrass, Gunn, Wilbur, Kennedy—and the list goes on into the present generation. Looking back over the postwar years, one can make a good case that the poems with the greatest staying power were in fact written in meter, but even those who would debate that point must concede the remarkable gains in idiomatic grace and range of expression made by writers using traditional tools.

And now that the pendulum has started to swing back, journals favoring meter are springing up, and even mainstream publications like the *New Yorker* and *Poetry* are willing, albeit inconsistently, to offer space to poems written in form. With encouragement and a new tenuous sense of equal opportunity in the air, younger writers are once again training their ears to the subtle but infectious music of what was once the resistance. As they do so they may be unaware just how far their mentors moved while appearing to stand fast.

NOTES

Portions of this chapter appeared in the introduction to my earlier book *Sparring with the Sun* (2013), but I believe their relevance to the material in this section justifies their revival.

1. Stephen Berg and Robert Mezey, Introduction to *Naked Poetry* (Bobbs-Merrill, 1969).

2. *On Poetry and Poetics* (Faber, 1957), p. 159. Cited in Steele, *Missing Measures* (University of Arkansas Press, 1990), p. 33.

3. *To Criticize the Critic* (Farrar Straus, 1965), pp. 188–89. Quoted in Steele, p. 94.

4. "Preface," *Quarterly Review of Literature*, II:4 (1944), p. 349.

5. "Experimental and Formal Verse: Some Hints toward the Enjoyment of Modern Verse," *Quarterly Review of Literature*, VII:3 (1953), p. 174.

6. Here is Olson on form: "Absolute bull/shit. That is: the intelligence that had touted Auden as being a technical wonder, etc. Lacking all grip on the worn and useless character of his essence: thought. An attitude that puts weight, *first:* on form/more than say: what you have above: will never get to: content. Never in god's world. Anyhow, form has now become so useless a term/ that I blush to use it. I wd imply a little of Stevens' use (the things created *in* a poem and existing there . . .) & too, go over into: the possible casts of method for a way into/a 'subject': to make it clear: that form is never more than an *extension* of content." "Projective Verse," *Poetry New York*, no. 3 (1950), pp. 78–79.

7. Poetry Foundation biographic note on Williams: http://www.poetryfoundation.org/bio /william-carlos-williams

8. *Blank Verse* (Ohio University Press, 2007), p. 152.

9. From the introduction. The mention of "duration" of a foot suggests confusion with the foot employed in classical (Latin and Greek) scansion, but in fact the editors chose poems that for the most part avoided ordinary English iambics. That is not to say there wasn't frequent flirtation with form. Mezey's own contributions included an unmetered and unrhymed sonnet and a humorous poem, also unmetered, that employs half-rhymes throughout, to good effect.

10. Annie Finch, *The Ghost of Meter: Culture and Prosody in American Free Verse* (University of Michigan Press, 1993).

11. *Blank Verse*, p. 242.

13

PUTTING ON THE STYLE

(1) Subject, identified by witnesses as Malachi ("Buck") Mulligan, appeared to be in his mid-twenties and was of stocky build. He was seen at the top of the stairway advancing deliberately while carrying a bowl containing a frothy substance, possibly shaving lather. One witness said that a mirror and a razor lay at angles across the rim of the bowl. Subject was clad in a yellow (silk?) bathrobe which was untied and frequently fluttered behind him. He was observed to raise the bowl above eye-level, apparently in imitation of a priest conducting mass. . . .

(2) Yes, I saw him and I knew right away who he was. He was my brother's friend Buck Mulligan—this heavy-set dreamboat who's in medical school. He was staying in this tower with some friends, and he had apparently just got up. He comes up the stairs with this basin and shaving stuff and he's putting on a show, you know? He's got this yellow silk bathrobe he hasn't even bothered to tie, and it's floating out behind him, and he hoists up the bowl of lather with the mirror and razor and makes like he's a priest celebrating mass. I almost died laughing. . . .

Here are two accounts of the same event, each allowing a reader to imagine a fair amount about the nature and character of the reporter while also picturing the scene in the mind's eye. What makes that possible is the style of the narration: the first relies heavily on passive-voice sentences making a show of noncommittal objectivity. The second manages through word choice and small additions to convey a girlish, confiding, sexualized tone.

Contrast these accounts, which I've invented, with that of Buck Mulligan's creator, who opined that "the artist, like the god of the creation, remains within or behind or beyond or above his handiwork, invisible, refined out of existence, indifferent, paring his fingernails." "Stately, plump Buck Mulligan came from the stairhead, bearing a bowl of lather on which a mirror and a razor lay crossed. A yellow dressing gown, ungirdled, was sustained gently behind him by the mild morning air. He held the bowl aloft. . . ."[1] Yet even the god of the creation, it seems, leaves behind him some telling identifiers. We all know what a *stairhead* is; it is defined in the *Oxford English Dictionary*. But the OED's American counterpart, Webster's *Third International,* omits it, while including *staircase, stairway,* and *stairwell.* We know, too, what a dressing gown is, though few people today would look for one in their closet.[2] On both sides of the Atlantic the word *girdled* is chiefly used metaphorically (as in a hill girdled by trees), and *ungirdled* appears in the OED only as a synonym for *ungirded*—that is, divested of military gear. So we may conclude that the author of the passage came from the British Isles, likely lived at a time when people commonly spoke of *dressing gowns,* and had a punctilious regard for the literal and figurative meanings of words. But it is the word *sustained* in that second sentence that gives away his genius. "Sustain" is an abstract word in most people's speech, meaning "to keep (something) going," but its Latin ancestor meant literally "to hold (something) up," and when it comes to us in that sentence—"sustained . . . by the mild morning air"—its ancient meaning lights up in our minds.

Where there is language there is necessarily style—of expression with precision, grace, and balance perhaps—but also of subterfuge: elaborating, qualifying, or even undercutting the ostensible message.

I want to look at the various guises of verbal style, the elements of language that writers manipulate to produce a style, and the ways readers react when they encounter them. Styles, as we all know, go in and out of fashion; to be effective they depend on an audience attuned to their peculiarities. Just as we appraise someone's discourse not only by its paraphrasable content but also by the tone of voice in which it is spoken, by the pronunciation of words ("accent"), and by the speed of its delivery, so we make numerous micro-judgments of the *written* information we absorb.

In some cases styles can affect content: certain styles are suited to some kinds of meaning but not to others. Thus, one who introduces a new style may bring a new set of concerns along with it. If the innovations become popular, it's hard to say whether that was because of style or content—or both.

To make all this more explicit, consider the elements of language that constitute style.

Lexical Level

At the lexical level, such elements involve word choice (formal, informal, slangy or dialectal), word sound (end-rhyme, internal rhyme, consonance, alliteration), syllable count (sometimes), and stress pattern (meter). Also the absence of attention to these things.

Leaving aside meter, rhyme, and the division of speech into lines, consider these three prose instances:

> The Widow Douglas she took me for her son, and allowed she would sivilize me; but it was rough living in the house all the time, considering how dismal regular and decent the widow was in all her ways; and so when I couldn't stand it no longer I lit out.[3]

> Once a bitch always a bitch, what I say. I says you're lucky if her playing out of school is all that worries you.[4]

> My legal name is Alexander Perchov. But all of my many friends dub me Alex, because that is a more flaccid-to-utter version of my legal name. Mother dubs me Alexi-stop-spleening-me!, because I am always spleening her.[5]

Just a few changes from standard English characterize the rural Southern speech of Huck Finn: the pronoun after "Widow Douglas"; "allowed" instead of "vowed"; the dropping of the adverbial ending in "dismal regular"; "no longer" for "any longer"; and the colloquial "lit out." These adjustments are enough to tell us his social class and level of education; his observations will soon convince us of his perceptiveness and his empathy.

Jason Compson's misogyny and bitterness come through immediately in his word choice. The words are evidently spoken aloud, either to a captive audience or to himself. "What I say" and "I says" are colloquial expressions used by half-educated people in his milieu. In this case they emphasize the self-centered and self-pitying character of the speaker.

Alex Perchov's first words mark him as bookish and inward-looking but with a hint of a capacity to be amused at his own behavior. They also identify him as someone who learned English laboriously with the aid of a dictionary and a thesaurus, someone who seems to have a genius for finding the most esoteric possible word to convey the simple meaning he intends.

All this information about the character and social position of the speakers is conveyed instantly by their style of speech, in the first two or three sentences they utter.

A different kind of information is added when sentences are measured out in light and heavy syllables and marked at intervals by like-ending words—in short when we enter the realm of poetry. Consider this passage of prose: "Sonia, Cecilia—where the mountain river meets the brook, and Lafayette and Gale blur in shallow confluence, and silver minnows court you both: with net and pail one of you wades beneath the branches, netting little fish; the other dams the still bright water, lifting stones and briefly fretting rings in the brook. The sun stands on the hill." It's a lovely descriptive passage, situating the scene at the juncture of two rivers in New Hampshire, the time in summer, and the girls (aided by the title, "Eleven") on the cusp of adolescence. Now see how much more compelling it becomes when metered as the author intended:

> Sonia, Cecilia—where the mountain river
> meets the brook, and Lafayette and Gale
> blur in shallow confluence, and silver
> minnows court you both: with net and pail,
> one of you wades beneath the branches, netting
> little fish; the other dams the still
> bright water, lifting stones and briefly fretting
> rings in the brook. The sun stands on the hill.[6]

The minute pauses at the line-endings slow down the description. They are gently reinforced by rhymes made less noticeable and less emphatic than they might be because they occur, most of them, in the middle of a phrase where the speaking voice would not naturally stop (that is, the lines are enjambed). The effect is to give reflective attention to a scene that we might otherwise pass over quickly, allowing us to savor it without exaggerating its importance.

Contrast this effect with that of another rhymed passage, this one in tetrameter lines rhymed in couplets:

> Too frail to swim, she nonetheless
> Gingerly lifts her cotton dress
> Clear of the lake, so she can wade
> Where the descending sun has laid
> A net of rippling, molten bands
> Across the underwater sands.[7]

Here most of the phrase ends coincide with line-ends, and the rhymes become much more noticeable, a decisive part of the poem. These observations point to the fine degree of control that the stylistic devices of rhyme and meter give the writer over the content presented. Such control determines with considerable precision the reader's emotional and intellectual understanding of the matter at hand.

But in making these observations we find ourselves moving beyond isolated words and into a concern with phrases.

Phrasal Level

At the level of the phrase or sentence, style may involve repetition, word order (standard or typical and various departures therefrom), all the classical rhetorical devices (simile and metaphor, parallelism, chiasmus, hyperbole, synecdoche, etc.), grammatical tense, and the extensive possible varieties of sentence structure, length, and complexity.

Several of these devices, particularly repetition, are at play in Robert Frost's famous fourteen-liner:

> I have been one acquainted with the night.
> I have walked out in rain—and back in rain.
> I have outwalked the furthest city light.
>
> I have looked down the saddest city lane.
> I have passed by the watchman on his beat
> And dropped my eyes, unwilling to explain.
>
> I have stood still and stopped the sound of feet
> When far away an interrupted cry
> Came over houses from another street,

But not to call me back or say good-bye;
And further still at an unearthly height,
One luminary clock against the sky

Proclaimed the time was neither wrong nor right.
I have been one acquainted with the night.

　—"Acquainted with the Night"

The repeated phrases occur in half of the poem's lines (in fact the last line is a duplicate of the first), while other repetitive patterns occur in interior phrases: "out in rain—and back in rain"; "walked out," "outwalked"; "the furthest," "the saddest." There is also alliteration and internal rhyme: "stood *still* and *stopped*" (which chimes with "dropped" in the previous line)—all this while maintaining a terza rima pattern throughout the sonnet.

The repeated "I have"s stand as a sort of confession, enumerating a series of apparent transgressions. But this is not quite a confession; it is a lament and a statement of melancholy fact. That is the poem's denotative meaning, even as the confessional style casts a pall of regret over the entire discourse.

The importance of style in phrasing is heightened when a poem dispenses with rhyme and meter. Then repetition and contrast become paramount structuring devices. Here is the start of Louise Glück's "The Empty Glass":

I asked for much; I received much.
I asked for much; I received little, I received
next to nothing.

And between? A few umbrellas opened indoors.
A pair of shoes by mistake on the kitchen table.

O wrong, wrong—it was my nature. I was
hard-hearted, remote. I was
selfish, rigid to the point of tyranny.

The first line pairs two phrases of similar structure. The second starts the same, but with a shift in the second phrase, followed by a similar phrase that carries over to the third line. So a kind of chant becomes a form of catechism or self-analysis. The fourth and fifth lines abandon rhetoric for colloquial expressions of folk wisdom suggesting reasons for bad luck. But the next three lines, again colloquial in tone, reject that consolation: it was not bad luck that was responsible for the speaker's misfortune, but her character flaws: lines seven and eight each identify a moral failing. Repetitive phrasing recurs in the last tercet to reinforce the self-indictments: "wrong, wrong"; "I was / hard-hearted, remote"; "I was / selfish, rigid." The poem goes out of its way to position these similarly phrased accusations prominently. It becomes, like many of Glück's poems, a vehicle for unsparing self-scrutiny, examining her childhood as well as her adult avatar.

She ends with a contradiction: she asserts that "what is crucial is to believe / in effort, to believe some good will come of simply trying." But she also harks back to the legend of Agamemnon, insisting he was wrong to think his fate could be controlled. "He should have said / I have nothing, I am at your mercy." In this case we have two contrary ideas set against each other and unresolved. That too is a stylistic maneuver, but on a conceptual, not a linguistic level.

Conceptual Level

And that brings us to the conceptual realm, where stylistic options include establishing and changing points of view, sequencing narrated events, and choosing to use, distort, or abandon sequential reasoning. At this level you can see that manner begins to trespass on matter, for clearly how (or whether) one reasons will affect the substance one can convey.

Up to now I have been discussing poems that laid down a traceable train of thought, in which one could discern how one idea led to another. This is not to say that each idea followed logically from the preceding one; a poem is not a syllogism, and much of the delight a reader encounters stems from the surprising juxtaposition of two apparently unrelated perceptions. To take a famous example, William Carlos Williams spends eight stanzas of "The Yachts" describing the burnishing of boats in preparation for a race:

Mothlike in mists, scintillant in the minute

brilliance of cloudless days, with broad bellying sails
they glide to the wind tossing green water
from their sharp prows while over them the crew crawls

ant-like, solicitously grooming them . . .

But the ninth stanza awakens us to a shockingly different scene:

> Arms with hands grasping seek to clutch at the prows.
> Bodies thrown recklessly in the way are cut aside.
> It is a sea of faces about them in agony, in despair
>
> until the horror of the race dawns staggering the mind;
> the whole sea become an entanglement of watery bodies
> lost to the world bearing what they cannot hold.

. . . and we realize that the poem is about more than a boat race; it is about a destructive class divide, one that threatens not just the livelihoods but the lives of whole populations.

In Williams's poem the abrupt change is entirely on a conceptual level. The roughly five-beat tercets, like the lapping waves of the sea, proceed as smoothly in the shocking new reality as in the old. That is part of the reason the last part of the poem startles its readers.

But more typically, a change in mode of thought is signaled by a change in verse style. Such techniques were first developed in the theater. Shakespeare dramatizes several kinds of awareness in Act III of *King Lear*, signaled by changes in meter and vocabulary. Initially, even when thrust unprotected into the storm, Lear keeps his senses and speaks in blank verse:

> This tempest will not give me leave to ponder
> On things would hurt me more—But I'll go in.

Edgar, in disguise, feigns an unhinged paranoia by speaking in snatches of old rhymes:

> Away! The foul fiend follows me!—
> Through the sharp hawthorn blows the cold wind.—
>
> Hum! go to thy cold bed and warm thee.
> . . .
> Pillicock sat on Pillicock-hill:—
> Halloo, halloo, loo, loo!

The Fool, speaking prose, becomes the only voice of reason: "Prithee, nuncle, be contented; 'tis a naughty night to swim in.—Now a little fire in the wild field were like an old lecher's heart,—a small spark, all the rest on's body cold."

Later, Lear's abandonment of blank verse seems to signal his descent into madness, but it is a madness of sudden self-awareness: "When the rain came to wet me once, and the wind to make me chatter; when the thunder would not peace at my bidding; there I found 'em, there I smelt 'em out. Go to, they are not men o' their words; they told me I was everything; 'tis a lie,—I am not ague-proof."

The technique need not be confined to the stage. A hundred years ago "The Waste Land" earned part of its notoriety by its unnerving use of such verse disruptions.

> White bodies naked on the low damp ground
> And bones cast in a little low dry garret,
> Rattled by the rat's foot only, year to year,
> But at my back from time to time I hear
> The sound of horns and motors, which shall bring
> Sweeney to Mrs. Porter in the spring.
> O the moon shone bright on Mrs. Porter
> And on her daughter
> They wash their feet in soda water
> *Et o ces voix d'enfants, chantant dans la coupole!*
>
> Twit twit twit
> Jug jug jug jug jug jug
> So rudely forc'd.
> Tereu
>
> Unreal City
> Under the brown fog of a winter moon
> Mr. Eugenides, the Smyrna merchant
> Unshaven, with a pocket full of currants
> C.i.f. London: documents at sight,
> Asked me in demotic French
> To luncheon at the Cannon Street Hotel
> Followed by a weekend at the Metropole.

The passage begins with a description of an unappealing scene but segues in the fourth quoted line to words recalling Marvell's "To His Coy Mistress," then references a character (Sweeney) from an earlier poem of Eliot's and alludes to John Day's seventeenth-century poem "Parliament of Bees." All this happens in a loose blank verse. Then the meter shifts and parodies some World War I poetic doggerel, which is in turn a parody of a 1907 ballad called Redwing.[8] The last line in that section is a quotation from Verlaine's *Parsifal*. This is followed by a series of bird calls interspersed with a suggestion of the legend of Philomela, who was raped by Tereus (so rudely forc'd) and turned into a nightingale. The scene then shifts (while reverting to mostly blank verse) to an urban setting recalling a sleazy commercial transaction in which the un-identified speaker is propositioned by a Smyrna merchant.

There are numerous mysteries in Eliot's procedure. The shifts in tone and voice are only sometimes signaled by changes in meter, and the reason for the tonal shift is not always easy to see. Why does the verse sing of Sweeney and Mrs. Porter? What is the point of the reference to Philomela? Who is Mr. Eugenides and why is the encounter with him mentioned? All these feints and darts are oblique ways of dealing with what Eliot regarded as sexual degener-acy. In tune with the temper of the times, "The Waste Land" at once excited and mystified readers by declining to provide clear guides to meaning, instead planting both obscure and overt cultural references throughout the text. The reader's ingenuity must be brought to bear to make sense of the totality, and diverse readings are inevitable. Publication of the poem marked the begin-ning of an era that separated readers into two camps: in one are the critical and persistent readers who use reason and imagination to fathom a poet's concealed but evidently intended meaning (and often assist students in doing the same), and in the other, the much larger camp, are those who simply give up on "modern poetry" and gravitate to the poetic version of easy listening.[9]

A poetry rife with hints, suggestions, allusions, and mysterious references can speak of more than one thing at a time, as Eliot surely intended. But poets who become fascinated by the connotations and the sounds of words may start to abandon rational discourse altogether. There has long been a strain of ec-static irrationality in Romantic poetry, exemplified in Swinburne ("Ave Atque Vale," for example) and Hart Crane ("Voyages"), that tries to give voice to a generalized passion almost entirely freed from a motivating situation. Carried to extremes, the technique results in a poem strewn with clues, references, and images that suggest much and do not close in on anything. This is the stylistic signature of John Ashbery, who writes with a flippancy and ingenuity that have bedazzled and bedeviled legions of readers.[10] There is a kind of ingenuity to a sort of composition that sounds like cryptic wisdom but cannot be decoded to yield a consistent idea. I find it ultimately unsatisfying, like a crossword puzzle with clever clues but no right answers.

What we are seeing here—and it has become a template for much contemporary poetry—is a style that does not depend on the auditory properties of words (their sound, length, resemblances, etc.), or on the patterned arrangement of phrases, or on the deployment of classical rhetorical tropes, but rather on the artful scrambling of meanings to keep some suggestions hovering in the mind while preventing readers from saying, "Yes, I understand what he means." It leads to what I believe is an intellectual and artistic dead end, exemplified in the *Language* poets of our time.

But styles on the conceptual level can do more than lead readers down the paths through the elms, into the brilliant woods. A style can convey information, sometimes of a kind that cannot be couched in descriptive phrases. We saw information about character and background emerging in the quotations from Huckleberry Finn, Jason Compson, and Alexander Perchov. We see it most commonly in the dramatic monologue, where a speaker portrays himself, often indelibly, while discoursing on a matter that seemingly has nothing to do with confession or self-revelation.

Rosanna Warren, for example, has a poem called "Interior at Petworth" in which the hapless Lord Egremont laments what has become of his household since J. M. W. Turner was allowed to paint the house and grounds:

. . . Do not believe
I started this, it was
that man, who was to portray the park alone, mind you,
but then became
enamored of the music room.
And now what have we: floods
of fire rolling from room to room, furniture wrecked
in seethe, and my wife
Lady Amelia turned
wraith.

. . . .
He is a man
in love with last things, clearly,
the last things, but
never understood the first, it seems to me,
and certainly not the genial *medias res*
of decorous, daily life.
What tea-times we've known in these chambers, what sonatinas,
lieder of an evening, whist,
Emmeline embroidering, the hounds calm at the hearth, now all
dissolved. . . .

It is as if, as Nabokov's fictional psychologist noted in the preface to *Lolita*, an ape taught to paint had produced a sketch depicting the bars of its cage.

A final example, of a different sort: sometimes a received form—a codified style—can be applied to a subject in such a way as to illustrate and illuminate it as no amount of description could do. In "Shopping for Black Slacks," Margot Wizansky has taken the ancient form of the pantoum, a poem in four-line stanzas, in which the second and fourth lines in each stanza reappear as the first and third lines of the following stanza, and turned it into an enactment of the frightening onset of dementia.

At the boundary waters of her decline,
my mother decides she needs new black slacks.
So thin from salting her food, forgetting to eat,
I'm trying to find her what fits.

My mother's decided she needs new black slacks.
In the dressing room, she holds a pair in her hands.
I'm trying to find her what fits.
She can't remember if she's about to try them on

or take them off, the pair she holds in her hands.
She knew retail, high end. It was her life.
She can't remember if she's about to try them on,
slacks on the floor, on the chair, lopsided on hangers.

She knew retail, high end. It was her life.
Soon we find a rhythm—I hand her a pair—
slacks on the chair, the floor, on lopsided hangers—
she tries them—rejects them—I whisk them away—

soon we find a rhythm—I hand her a pair—
After she tries them, I give her another.
She tries them—rejects them—I whisk them away—
These fit! she says, the very pair she wore this morning.

I'm finished with giving her another pair to try.
So thin from salting her food, forgetting to eat,
these fit! she says, the very pair she wore this morning.
My mother's at the boundary waters of her decline.

To enact the perseveration that is often a manifestation of dementia, the poet has chosen a form based on perseveration: the relentless repetition of lines from one stanza to another. Not all instances of the pantoum form depict mental decline, of course. The form can be invoked for love poetry or to describe political or moral crises. But an alertness to the possible relation between this poetic form and this mental symptom allows the writer to bring forth one of its stylistic applications. By the time we get to the poem's final stanza, which repeats lines from the first, we feel we have experienced the boundary waters of the woman's decline. Through style we live the meaning.

．．．．

This leads to a final observation. Styles have fans. They become popular and they go *out of style*. That's as true of literature as of clothing. Whether by inheritance, by training, or by experience—or by some combination of these—people develop preferences for certain poetic conventions. Some readers are open to more than one style, but many have a pronounced preference for a narrow range. Such preferences are called "taste."[11] Taste is perhaps innate to some extent, but it is also learned; and once learned it may be broadened and sometimes deepened, but it is rarely altered fundamentally. One's taste becomes an essential part of who one is. At the same time, it's clear that not everyone is confident in his taste. Some people seek guidance. Some writers and critics, outspoken and articulate, become cultural arbiters and achieve a status that makes them trusted by many who doubt their own taste. The persistence of taste (of a certain kind) in audiences and journals keeps all but the boldest or most foolhardy poets from straying too far from the lanes established by their predecessors.

Out of such stylistic forays, errors, triumphs, and uneasy agreements we develop what we call tradition.

NOTES

1. James Joyce, *Ulysses* (Modern Library, 1922).

2. "Dressing gowns continued to be worn into the 20th century with similar garments like hostess dresses, robes, and peignoirs being used. However, dressing gowns began seeing less frequent usage later in the 20th century as wearing such garments became increasingly associated with idleness and lethargy. By the 21st century, dressing gowns have experienced little popularity and use." (Wikipedia.)

3. Mark Twain, *Huckleberry Finn* (Dover, 1994).

4. William Faulkner, Jason Compson in *The Sound and the Fury* (Modern Library, 1992).

5. Jonathan Safran Foer, *Everything Is Illuminated* (Houghton Mifflin, 2002).

6. Deborah Warren, "Eleven," *Zero Meridian* (Ivan R. Dee, 2004).

7. Timothy Steele, "Joanna, Wading," *Toward the Winter Solstice* (Swallow, 2006).

8.   Oh the moon shines bright on Mrs Porter
     And on her daughter,
     A regular snorter;
     She has washed her neck in dirty water
     She didn't oughter,
     The dirty cat.

Behind that is "Redwing" with words by Thurland Chattaway:

     Now the moon shines tonight on pretty Red Wing,
     The breeze is sighing, the night bird's crying,
     For afar 'neath his star her brave is sleeping,
     While Red Wing's weeping her heart away.

9. The ever-popular M.O.

10. See a more extensive analysis of Ashbery's writing in chapter 2, "Some Poetic Strategies."

11. A writer who cultivates and refines his or her style is said to develop a *voice*. It's noteworthy that "voice" seeks to appeal to "taste"—as if the receiver's receptive sense is misaligned with the writer's mode of expression.

14

WHERE DO WE COME FROM?
WHAT ARE WE? WHERE ARE WE GOING?

Paul Gauguin wrote those questions on his monumental canvas, painted while living in Tahiti in 1897. They are not questions an artist asks while practicing in a widely accepted tradition among peers who share largely the same values. Gauguin was moving away from Impressionism and toward a style that became known as Primitivism. The change was not as radical as the artistic, literary, and poetic shift that overtook Europe and America a few years after his death in 1903, but it was disruptive nevertheless, and his evidently heartfelt questions still apply to our moment and our verbal art, and still demand answers.

Where Do We Come From?

We are now more than a hundred years past the time when Pound and Eliot, Doolittle and Williams, and their rivals and associates caught the attention of readers and critics by declaring—and demonstrating—that poems could be written without meter or rhyme and sometimes with a language and meanings largely opaque to the ordinary reader. Since that time a vigorous tradition of nonmetrical poetry has arisen, with the result that many people can no longer hear meter, do not consider it a necessary part of a poem, and may even prefer poems that avoid it. Editors of many journals and magazines, including some reaching the widest audiences, either shun metrical and rhyming poetry altogether or display a few examples of it along with many of what is now the standard type.

But the takeover was not complete. Like the Norman conquest of 1066, it left a sturdy peasantry still habituated to the traditional speech, in this case metrical writing, often with rhyme and sometimes with other musical elements like alliteration. And like the common folk of a millennium ago, the metrical poets borrowed some features of the conquerors' idiom: in this case more colloquial speech, looser meter, less strident rhyme. As a result, we currently have two traditions of poetry operating in parallel, each with its own journals, book publishers, and exemplary champions. The current dominance of nonmetrical poetry is not necessarily a permanent fixture of the literary landscape. Both traditions are vigorous, and there is talent on both sides. Here I am interested in a closer analysis of the differences as a way of perhaps charting the course to come.

As I suggested with the introductory remarks on Gauguin, there are parallels between the revolution in the graphic arts and that in poetry. The parallels are made explicit in an intriguing poem recently published by John Foy called "At Sea (*after paintings by Piet Mondrian*)":

> The pier and ocean. What has happened here?
> What freedom is it that we've won
> now the ocean overwhelms the pier?
> The pier is gone, or almost gone,
> the lines that it was made of more or less
> disaggregated now till all we have
> are plus and minus signs, a meaningless
> eolian effect upon the waves.
> Is this what we've become? No sun,
> no sky, no water we're familiar with,
> only broken-up geometry
> that bears no trace of what we'd been.
> We left the pier behind, what it was worth
> we didn't know, and now we are at sea.

It's useful to know that Mondrian began as a representational painter but embraced abstract work as he developed and ultimately became one of abstraction's foremost representatives, using rectilinear forms and vivid colors. The sonnet, written by a poet adept at handling traditional meters and rhymes, expresses regret for what has been lost by the erasure of the manmade structures that give order and meaning to the welter of nature. There is little in the poem to suggest that Mondrian's later work is highly regular and structured, albeit nonrepresentational.

Indeed, in their distress at the loss of the constraints of meter and rhyme in verse (and the loss of a real-world referent in painting), traditionalists often regard the newer, now dominant kinds of art as formless.[1] But are "formless" poems the same as prose? Not necessarily. Recall that the formal devices of meter and rhyme are aspects of natural language that are ordered so that they recur regularly and create a discernible rhythm. In particular, the selected features in English are syllables and stress (the basis for meter)[2] and vowel-consonant sound (the basis for rhyme). If we cease to control these, is there anything left that can give a sense of regularity—a pulse—and thus an emotional boost to an utterance? Indeed there is, and it is one of the oldest means of creating pattern and force in most languages. This device is the repetition of words and of similar grammatical phrases, and it is as old as the Hebrew Bible:

> A time to be born, a time to die;
> a time to plant, and a time to pluck up that which is planted;
> A time to kill, and a time to heal;
> a time to break down, and a time to build up;
> A time to weep, and a time to laugh;
> a time to mourn, and a time to dance . . .

This is not poetry as it was formalized in the long English tradition,[3] but it is also not prose in the narrative or expository manner. It is a special kind of high rhetoric, long familiar to those raised in the western tradition, and of course available to the avant garde poets who had jettisoned meter and rhyme.

Not all of them used it all the time. Short poems in short lines with vivid details (a red wheelbarrow, petals on a wet black bough) could be written without even this much patterning, but when William Carlos Williams essayed slightly longer works, like "By the Road to the Contagious Hospital," quoted in chapter 12, he called on the age-old tradition. Readers can find there a number of repeated words and closely related phrases in a dozen lines: *brown, standing, tall trees / small trees, leafless / lifeless.*

The device, known by rhetoricians as parataxis with anaphora, was extensively and famously used in poems by Walt Whitman but was rediscovered and popularized by most of the iconic rebels against traditional forms in the early twentieth century:

> What thou lovest well remains,
>
> the rest is dross
> What thou lov'st well shall not be reft from thee
> What thou lov'st well is thy true heritage
> Whose world, or mine or theirs
>
> or is it of none?
>
> —Ezra Pound, "Canto LXXXI"

> April is the cruellest month, breeding
> Lilacs out of the dead land, mixing
> Memory and desire, stirring
> Dull roots with spring rain.
> Winter kept us warm, covering
> Earth in forgetful snow, feeding
> A little life with dried tubers.
>
> —T. S. Eliot, "The Waste Land"

It is self-evidently an endlessly flexible and capable technique. Patterns can occur within patterns, as in the Williams passage and often in Eliot. Repetitive sequences need not occur in the same part of a line. Words, phrases, or complete sentences can be repeated, either literally or by grammatical form or type. By midcentury and the advent of a new generation of Beat poets, it was an accepted style of nonmetrical verse:

> angelheaded hipsters burning for the ancient heavenly connection to the
>   starry dynamo in the machinery of night,
> who poverty and tatters and hollow-eyed and high sat up smoking in the
>   supernatural darkness of cold-water flats floating across the tops of cities
>   contemplating jazz,

<u>who</u> bared their brains to Heaven under the El and saw Mohammedan angels
   staggering on tenement roofs illuminated,

<u>who</u> passed through universities with radiant cool eyes hallucinating
   Arkansas and Blake-light tragedy among the scholars of war,

<u>who</u> were expelled from the academies for crazy & publishing obscene odes
   on the windows of the skull,

<u>who</u> cowered in unshaven rooms in underwear, burning their money in
   wastebaskets and listening to the Terror through the wall, . . .

—Allen Ginsberg, "Howl"

Line length did not matter: no one was counting syllables or stresses. What mattered—what controlled audience response—was the repeated cue word or phrase that generated expectation, reassurance, and cumulative excitement all at once. Pound had said "Make it new!" but he might with more justice have advised "Make it old!"—for the rhetorical technique was more ancient than Cicero, and it was proving to be as generative as ever.[4]

I do not want to overstate the case. This new-old technique of imposing form on language did not become as essential a feature of the new poetry as meter had once been of the old. Shorter poems are often written without it; longer ones often use it intermittently; whether by design or by unconscious recourse is hard to say. But one can hardly dip into recent issues of *Poetry* magazine, which under its current editorship has accepted little verse in meter and rhyme, without finding poems relying heavily on repetition.

. . . .

Of course we are not dealing only with verse forms. The much larger issue is how—or whether—a poem may be understood. Increasingly over the last several decades, critics and practicing poets have challenged the traditional concept of a poem as a vehicle for conveying or exploring a rational argument, a set of related impressions, or an emotion, whether recollected in tranquility or otherwise. By freeing language from the constraints of grammar and treating words as atoms of meaning that can be variously moved about on the canvas of the page, whole schools of poets have enlarged or fragmented the idea of poetry while at the same time narrowing its audience.[5] Stephen (now

Stephanie) Burt, a critic generally sympathetic to such styles, offers some tips on how to approach poems of this kind:

> The most important precepts are the simplest: look for a persona and a world, not for an argument or a plot. Enjoy double meanings: don't feel you must choose between them. Ask what the disparate elements have in common. . . . Look for self-analyses or for frame-breaking moments. . . . Look for the patterns you might seek in visual art. Especially if a poem avoids grammatical sense—if it looks like a canvas strewn with phrases—try treating it as if it were such a canvas. . . . If some poems resemble pieces of visual art, other poems resemble games whose rules you can learn. . . . Contemporary poems like these hold together if we can imagine a personality behind them. The poem carries, as people do, a social or regional or ethnic context; it leaps, as a person's thoughts do, from topic to topic, and it lacks, as real people usually lack, a single story line or motive that defines it.[6]

Elsewhere, Burt likens such poems to unassembled furniture that lacks instructions for putting it together. Readers may enjoy intuiting the instructions or making up their own. Or they may resign in frustration and search instead for poems already assembled by acknowledged craftsmen.

Some theorists have gone so far as to assert that this kind of do-it-yourself poetry demands a different kind of intelligence in the audience or viewer. Aware that the interpretation of grammatical speech calls on a deeply ingrained part of our neural structure, the linguist Samuel Jay Keyser asserts in a recent book that, with the advent of modernism, "General intelligence took over from hard-wired proclivity." We had to think, he says, with the more analytic part of the brain in order to understand this newer kind of writing. "When the brain came up against its natural limits, it had to resort to a different way of thinking. . . . Modernism and post-Newtonian science were both part and parcel of the same thing: the brain relinquishing its natural proclivities for the products of general intelligence."[7]

It may be that some conceptual features of modern poems call for what Keyser calls a new application of general intelligence instead of whatever people used to rely on to understand poems. But it is clear that perceiving and responding to repeated words and grammatical patterns places no new demands on the brain. In fact, by freeing readers or hearers of poetry from the need to process rhythmic and rhyming patterns concurrently with grammatical structures, modernist poets were in some cases making it easier for them to take in what they heard. In compensation they often complicated the communication by making logical connections more tenuous or removing them altogether, thus putting a premium on the perceiver's ingenuity in supplying or inventing them. Whether this ingenuity calls on a previously untapped form of general intelligence is a matter for debate or—perhaps better—for neurological research.

To tie this question of content back to our preoccupation with form, I will note the obvious: poems written in meter or with a prominent rhythm tend to be rational and understandable. Those that forsake meter may still present a clear thought line and often exhibit subtle and sensitive analysis, as in the work of Louise Glück. But most contemporary poems that depart from rational structures also depart from meter.

What Are We?

For some time now, poets have fallen into two ill-assorted camps. One consists of those who abjure the use of meter (usually) and of rhyme (almost always) but who have no principled objection to other rhetorical techniques, including phrasal repetition. These poets tend to stray far, deliberately or otherwise, from the rational, linear development of images and ideas. The other, somewhat smaller group is made up of writers who believe poems should be metrical, who naturally compose in meter, and who have no principled objection to rhyme, though many expand the concept to embrace words that share a final consonant but not a final vowel sound (*flight* and *thought*) or, less often, the other way around (*flight* and *spike*). Their style of exposition tends to be more traditional. Most magazines and many anthologies choose sides between so-called formalists and partisans of what is somewhat misleadingly called free verse.

This gives us a partial answer to the question What Are We? But it is not the whole answer, for it neglects the powerful social force embodied in rap or hip hop poetry. Growing out of the neighborhood contests between young men who vied to surpass each other with the ingenuity of their insults, rap became a vehicle for challenge, protest, social commentary, and more.[8] While still carrying the aura of popular entertainment, it began to assume many of the functions traditionally associated with poetry.

Rap poetry has a beat—often accompanied and emphasized by drums—but it is not metered in a classical sense. The number of unstressed syllables between stressed ones can vary widely, depending on the tempo and the material being spoken. The stressed syllables, however, are frequently rhymed—at least one to a line, sometimes more, and often rhymes occur within the same line. The rhymes are not exact: they aim for similar vowel sounds but only sometimes match consonants. However, they are often polysyllabic and involve two or more words.

As for content, it has been steadily broadening. From its origins as a weapon of dueling verbal wits, rap has evolved to include evocative depictions of the physical and moral environments inhabited by its users. Tradition-minded observers who are distressed by the grittiness of the landscape rap depicts might look back at T. S. Eliot for comparison—

> The yellow fog that rubs its back upon the window-panes,
> The yellow smoke that rubs its muzzle on the window-panes,
> Licked its tongue into the corners of the evening,
> Lingered upon the pools that stand in drains,
> Let fall upon its back the soot that falls from chimneys,
> Slipped by the terrace, made a sudden leap,
> And seeing that it was a soft October night,
> Curled once about the house, and fell asleep.
> And indeed there will be time
> For the yellow smoke that slides along the street,
> Rubbing its back upon the window-panes;
> There will be time, there will be time
> To prepare a face to meet the faces that you meet;
> There will be time to murder and create . . .
>
> —"The Love Song of J. Alfred Prufrock"

—and find much the same setting, with a lurking sense of danger and only slightly franker language, in a rap of similar length by Talib Kweli:

> Breathing in deep city breaths, sitting on shitty steps
> We stoop to new lows, hell froze the night the city slept

The beast crept through concrete jungles
Communicating with one another
And ghetto birds where waters fall
From the hydrants to the gutters
The beast walk the beats, but the beats we be making
You on the wrong side of the track, looking visibly shaken

. . . . .

Look in the skies for God, what you see besides the smog
Is broken dreams flying away on the wings of the obscene
Thoughts that people put in the air
Places where you could get murdered over a glare
But everything is fair
It's a paradox we call reality
So keeping it real will make you casualty of abnormal normality

    —"Respiration"[9]

Kweli, a rapper from a family of academics, might have chosen to publish poems in the usual journals and join the ranks of aspiring writers hoping to make their way into the anthologies. Instead he has issued rap videos that reach a different but much wider audience. It remains to be seen if the audiences devoted to the two modes of expression—written and oral—will coalesce. The wide popularity of the musical *Hamilton*, which employs the hip hop style throughout but which its audience can read as well as hear, suggests that they might.

Where Are We Going?

To sum up the status of poetry at this moment, we can say the art (if it is indeed one art) is practiced in several ways, with some poets eschewing meter and rhyme, some embracing both, some approaching rhyme gingerly, intermittently, or inventively, and most making use of phrasal repetition to command attention, heighten interest, and generate excitement. Poets vary widely in the degree to which they allow their verse to follow a discernible line of thought. For some, logical structure is a prerequisite; for others it is the mark of a conventional mind and something to be avoided. On the whole it appears that a large part of the current zeitgeist is sympathetic toward suggestive phrases and fleeting references that evoke flashes of memory or feeling almost as dreams do, without ever crystalizing into clear description or coherent argument. As Marjorie Perloff, one of the critics most sympathetic to experimental trends among once-marginalized groups, observes,

> My own sense is that the transformation that has taken place in verse may well be more generational than it is gendered. We have, in any case, a poetics of non-linearity or post-linearity that marks, not a return to the "old forms," . . . but a kind of "afterimage" of earlier soundings. . . . The new poems are, in most cases, as visual as they are verbal; they must be seen as well as heard, which means that at poetry readings, their scores must be performed, activated. Poetry, in this scheme of things, becomes what McCaffery has called "an experience in language rather than a representation by it."[10]

Since Perloff wrote that essay, two decades ago, the anticoherence movement in one segment of the poetic universe has coalesced and worked to develop its own theories. One exponent is poet Andrew Joron, who became fascinated by Leonardo da Vinci's "Deluge" drawings and writings and worked to tie them to a contemporary aesthetic.

> The representation of complex, irregular motion in the Deluge drawings fore-shadowed a new poetics of vision and a new understanding of nature whose significance is only beginning to be understood in our own time, especially in light of abstract and nonrepresentational art on the one hand, and the new science of chaos and complexity theory on the other. . . . Once poetic language was released from the constraint of having to tell the stories of gods and kings and later, of having to express individual and social identity, it began to discover— or rediscover—its sources in the mysterious movement of language itself, in the manifestation of a meaning in words that goes somehow beyond words. In the modernist and the postmodernist poem, language is finally manifested as a self-exceeding system. . . . A simple system, such as a clock or a pendulum, is not capable of such transformation; only complex, nonlinear systems are. Water and language are both classic examples of complex systems, and as such they have many properties in common—properties that, for me, relate directly to poetic attempts to say the unsayable.[11]

WHERE DO WE COME FROM? WHAT ARE WE? WHERE ARE WE GOING?

And what is the unsayable? Perhaps we'll know it when we see it. Several ideas appear to lurk behind this aesthetic. One is that everything that can be expressed (and is worth saying) has already been said. Another (irrefutable) is that there are great mysteries we have not begun to penetrate. A third is that our world is fathomless and overwhelming, and the best we can do is lob words at it in the forlorn hope of a response. (This, I'll note parenthetically, is the theme of Robert Frost's poem "The Most of It.") A corollary is that language used in this way becomes a kind of word game in which patterns take precedence over meaning.

How does this aesthetic work in practice? Contemporary poetry, as you can imagine, is all over the lot, but much in the currently popular mode appears in *Poetry* magazine, from a recent issue of which I've culled two examples. The first employs grammar, the second largely does not. Here is an excerpt from "now" by Aditi Machado:

> at the borders of systems always something a bit extra
> like beyond the slash of begonia an ancillary, almost
> bitter, pink—there <u>linger</u> there <u>drugged out</u>
> on phenotypical essences, craven & horny & hardwired
> for whatever's on the brink splintering
> oranges erupting in odorous flame—<u>linger</u>
> by the exquisite corpse of this delay
> <u>dragged out</u> & fatally nervous
> & in the head derision roses
> you minister the <u>margins</u>
> of apoplectic reed, murmurs in the hearts of palms
> <u>a speed of thought</u> hitherto unrealized
> <u>a speed of access</u> to what's now
> where the <u>margin</u> of error is is[12]

Note the repeated phrases I have marked, which give some structure to a poem that avoids meter and rhyme. Note too that while there are strange ellipses here and there ("& in the head derision roses / you minister the margins"), by and large the grammar is tight enough to convey a real idea, namely that this observer finds the strongest impressions at the edge of things, whether images or events. The idea and the form in which it is expressed are clear enough to allow for a real debate over whether *this* form does a better job than a more traditional one might in bringing home the impact of the poet's perception.

The second example builds no sentences, instead using syntax only to create unanchored phrases for whatever their isolated meanings can convey:

roped in <u>incremen</u>tal ghost <u>tens</u>
    future <u>tens</u> clairvoyant <u>tens</u>   home <u>tens</u>

blue slips beneath the exposed wing
tilt then seam then an angle spent all inside
the distance between thumb and thimble and fingerprint

    height exceeds then brims
    makes a solvent of it

  what vaunted green excess enclosed in each skimmed year then the years
      vanquished any fuchsia sky
the excess leaking forward <u>filmed aqua</u>
          <u>filled aqua</u>

fastened by ulna by <u>increments of ten</u>
fortunes sidled with
what have we when we give the mandible the fragments by
    <u>tens</u>?

—Asiya Wadud, excerpt from "Mandible Wishbone Solvent"

Again I have flagged repeated words and phrases that attempt to give a sense of structure to the lines. It is questionable whether general intelligence, as opposed to our natural proclivities, can throw much light on this passage. Like many other poems of this kind, it stands as an experiment or test to see whether a durable literature can be created by breaking down language into malleable fragments.

A notable omission from most of the postmodernist discussions of poetry is the role of emotion. Traditionally, the language of poetry, both word choice and rhythmic structure, was aimed not just at informing the mind but at provoking a strong emotional response. Since emotion, to my knowledge, has not yet gone out of style, it is noteworthy that current poetic fashions have paid so little attention to the ways of conveying it in language. Perhaps such neglect is a response to the sentimentality of much poetry in earlier generations. Perhaps it is a defense against the debased and violent emotionalism of much contemporary culture. Perhaps some of rhetoric's ancient tools for arousing emotion await rediscovery.

Among the so-called formalists, who have not abandoned metrical struc-tures or discernible lines of thought in poems, emotion—even strong emotion—can still be found. These poets face a different problem: how to discover a new way of seeing, and a new access of feeling, that goes beyond what we have already encountered. One approach is to loosen but not abandon meter, while keeping alive the art of description and evocative language through metaphor and simile, as in this passage, in which poet Gregory Pardlo conjures up a girl jumping rope:

> How she dances
> patterns like a dust-heavy bee retracing
> its travels in scale before the hive. How
> the whole stunning contraption of girl and rope
> slaps and scoops like a paddle boat.
> Her misted skin arranges the light
> with each adjustment and flex. Now heather-
> hued, now sheen, light listing on the fulcrum
> of a wrist and the bare jutted joints of elbow
> and knee, and the faceted surfaces of muscle,
> surfaces fracturing and reforming
> like a sun-tickled sleeve of running water.
> She makes jewelry of herself and garlands
> the ground with shadows.

> —"Double Dutch"

. . . .

Between the schematic organization of an encyclopedia, at one extreme, and total incomprehensibility, at the other, there are of course infinitely many degrees, but it is evident that the communication of ideas, with associated attitudes and feelings, is not an objective universally shared among today's poets. Nevertheless, most laypeople still regard art as a form of communication, though admittedly the most receptive and perceptive ones may comprise only a small coterie.

Centuries of experience have taught us that it is not easy to communicate new insights in arresting ways that have a chance to be remembered by later generations. In our time this is not even a universal objective, as we have seen. Many writers are more interested in conversing and competing with a peer group; others aim to afflict the comfortable, still others follow (and misconstrue) Wittgenstein in regarding language as essentially a game. I would not disparage such aims, though I would observe that the extreme difficulty of a game is no reason to change the rules. But the relatively small cadre of poets who wish to make a lasting statement face difficult decisions: how far will the techniques of their forebears serve them in the future? What will get the attention of critics and other readers who have read a great deal, including poems of surpassing insight and beauty by writers of previous generations? Even assuming one has something new to say, is there a new way to say it? If they do nothing else, such questions may cause thoughtful poets to study the work of those who have gone before them, if only to learn and create what is truly new, while not being quick to dismiss the tools their foreparents have developed and refined.

NOTES

1. The parallel issues of nonrepresentational art and atonal music will have to be left for a more wide-ranging inquiry at a later time.

2. Stress in English is actually a complex phenomenon comprised partly of volume and partly of a change in pitch in relation to surrounding syllables. Prosodists who cannot precisely define it still maintain (along with untutored listeners) that they know it when they hear it.

3. Evidently feeling that they could and should be made into poetry, Mary Sidney Herbert and her brother Philip Sidney recast many of the Psalms into rhyming English verse.

4. Recent scientific research has pointed to a bias in nature toward repetitive and symmetrical structures. Luís Seoane, a complex systems researcher at the Centro Nacional de Biotecnología in Spain, observed that symmetrical structures simplify organic development and functioning: "There is a war going on between simplicity and complexity, and we live right at the edge of it." (Quoted in the *New York Times,* March 24, 2022.)

5. This is an unkind guess. The audience for poetry—as measured in book sales—is and always has been minuscule. To cite some random facts: Of the two thousand copies of the 1832 edition of Wordsworth's poems, fewer than four hundred had been sold by September 1833. James Joyce's

Chamber Music was published in 1907. By 1913, fewer than two hundred copies out of 507 printed had been bought, many, it is said, by Joyce.

6. Stephen Burt, *Close Calls with Nonsense* (Graywolf, 2009), 11–13.

7. Samuel Jay Keyser, *The Mental Life of Modernism: Why Poetry, Painting, and Music Changed at the Turn of the Twentieth Century* (MIT Press, 2021).

8. For a comprehensive description of the origins of rap and hip hop, see Jelani Cobb, *To the Break of Dawn* (New York University Press, 2007).

9. The entire rap was jointly written by Yasiin Bey (formerly known as Mos Def) and Talib Kweli. The portion I have quoted is by Kweli and is so identified in the online and printed lyrics.

10. *"After Free Verse: The New Non-Linear Poetries" in Poetry On & Off the Page: Essays for Emergent Occasions* (University of Alabama Press, 2004), citing Steve McCaffery, "Diminished Reference and the Model Reader," *North of Intention: Critical Writings 1973–1986* (Roof Books, 2000), who speaks of a poetry "without walls," in which "milieu and constellation replace syntax."

11. Andrew Joron, "Flowing Uphill" (essay on the Poetry Foundation website: https://www .poetryfoundation.org/articles/69139/flowing-uphill).

12. The term "exquisite corpse" in this poem harks back to a word game invented by French Surrealists a hundred years ago, in which players took turns choosing random words (sometimes following grammatical rules, sometimes not) to form fantastic phrases. A modern version, "Magnetic Poetry," is a game allowing players to arrange individual words (printed on magnetic strips) on the side of a refrigerator to achieve strange outcomes. Both procedures invoke chance as a stand-in for imagination.

Acknowledgments

The author is grateful to the editors of these journals for permission to reprint:

1. **"Sources of Delight: What We Respond to When We Respond to Poetry"**
   Not previously published.

2. **"Some Poetic Strategies"**
   Published in *Literary Imagination* 18.2 (2016) as "Some Mimetic Strategies"

3. **"The Elusive Self: Poems and Personas"**
   Published in *Literary Imagination* 22.2 (2020)

4. **"But Enough about Me: Poems without Personas"**
   Published in *Think* 8.2 (2018)

5. **"All in the Family: Parents and Children in Today's Poetry"**
   Published in *Literary Imagination* 22.1 (2020)

6. **"Short of Breath: Poems in a Narrow Compass"**
   Published in *Literary Matters,* 10.3 (2018)

7. **"The Phoenix Line: History of a Style"**
   Published in *Think* 5.2 (2015)

8. **"On the Translation of Poetry"**
   Published in *Think* 11.1 (2021)

ACKNOWLEDGMENTS

9. "Serpent in the Tree: Poetry of a Fallen World"
   Published in *Think* 10.1 (2020)

10. "The Curator as Oracle: A Guide to *The Harlem Gallery*"
   Published in *Literary Imagination* 24.1 (2022)

11. "Enter at Your Own Risk: Poems of Vijay Seshadri"
   Published in *Think* 11.2 (2021)

12. "Formalists against the Tide: What They Learned from the Tide"
   Adapted from the Introduction to *Sparring with the Sun* (2013)

13. "Putting on the Style"
   Published in *Literary Imagination* 26.1 (2024)

14. "Where Do We Come From? What Are We? Where Are We Going?"
   Published in *Think* 13.2 (2023)

Poetry Acknowledgments

"The Shampoo" from *Poems* by Elizabeth Bishop. Copyright © 2011 by The Alice H. Methfessel Trust. Publisher's Note and compilation copyright © 2011 by Farrar, Straus and Giroux. Reprinted by permission of Farrar, Straus and Giroux. All Rights Reserved.

"The Mirror" from *Collected Poems* by Edgar Bowers, copyright © 1997 by Edgar Bowers. Used by permission of Alfred A. Knopf, an imprint of the Knopf Doubleday Publishing Group, a division of Penguin Random House LLC. All rights reserved.

"The Pool Players: Seven at the Golden Shovel" from *The Essential Gwendolyn Brooks* (Library of America, 2005). Reprinted by consent of Brooks Permissions.

"I Know a Man" from *Selected Poems of Robert Creeley* by Robert Creeley. Copyright © 1991 by The Regents of the University of California. This material is used by permission of the University of California Press.

ACKNOWLEDGMENTS

"Actaeon" from *Hapax* by A. E. Stallings. Copyright © 2006 by A. E. Stallings. Used by permission of Northwestern University Press.

"Glut," from *Save the Last Dance* by Gerald Stern. Copyright © 2008 by Gerald Stern. Used by permission of W. W. Norton & Company, Inc.

"The Photograph." Copyright © 1987 by Ellen Bryant Voigt, from *Collected Poems* by Ellen Bryant Voigt. Used by permission of W. W. Norton & Company, Inc.

"Night Fishing" from *The Arkansas Testament* by Derek Walcott. Copyright © 1987 by Derek Walcott. Reprinted by permission of Farrar, Straus and Giroux. All Rights Reserved.

"Mind" from *New and Collected Poems* by Richard Wilbur. Copyright © 1947–1953; 1955–1988; Copyright © renewed 1975–1996 by Richard Wilbur. Used by permission of HarperCollins Publishers.

"Shopping for Black Slacks" from *The Yellow Sweater* by Margot Wizansky. Copyright © 2023 by Margot Wizansky. Used by permission of the author and Kelsay Books.

"Hurricane Song" from *Blue Laws: Selected and Uncollected Poems, 1995–2015* by Kevin Young, compilation copyright © 2016 by Kevin Young. Used by permission of Alfred A. Knopf, an imprint of the Knopf Doubleday Publishing Group, a division of Penguin Random House LLC. All rights reserved.

Editions of Poems Cited

Abbreviations

CB-FE   Charles Baudelaire, *Flowers of Evil*, ed. Marthiel Matthews and Jackson Matthews. New Directions, 1955.

EB-CP   Elizabeth Bishop, *The Complete Poems*. Farrar Straus, 1997.

ED-CP   *The Complete Poems of Emily Dickinson,* ed. Thomas Johnson. Little, Brown, 1961.

EGB   *The Essential Gwendolyn Brooks*, ed. Elizabeth Alexander. Library of America, 2005.

FG-SP   *Selected Poems of Fulke Greville*, ed. Thom Gunn. Faber, 1968.

HD-CP   *H.D.: Collected Poems 1912-1944,* ed. Louis Martz. New Directions, 1983.

JVC-CP   *The Poems of J. V. Cunningham*, ed. Timothy Steele. Swallow/Ohio University Press, 1997.

KR-NSP   *Kay Ryan, The Best of It: New and Selected Poems*. Grove, 2010.

LB-BE   *Louise Bogan, The Blue Estuaries*. Farrar Straus, 1968.

LG-P   *Louise Glück, Poems, 1962–2012*. Farrar Straus, 2013.

PL-CP   *Philip Larkin, Collected Poems*. Faber, 2003.

PPV   *The Poems of Paul Valéry*, translated by Jan Schreiber. Cambridge Scholars, 2021.

RF-CP   *The Poetry of Robert Frost*, ed. E. C. Lathem. Holt, 1968.

RL-CP   *Robert Lowell, Collected Poems*. Farrar Straus, 2003.

RW-CP   *Richard Wilbur, New and Collected Poems*. Harcourt Brace, 1988.

SP-CP   *Sylvia Plath, Collected Poems*. Harper, 1992.

TG-CP   *Thom Gunn, Collected Poems*. Farrar Straus, 1993.

TSE-CP   *T. S. Eliot, Collected Poems, 1909–1962*. Harcourt, 1963.

WBY-CP   *W. B. Yeats, Collected Poems*. Wadsworth Poetry Library, 1994.

WCW-CP   *Collected Poems of William Carlos Williams, Vol. 1: 1909–1939*. New Directions, 1991.

WDS-NSP   *W. D. Snodgrass, Not for Specialists: New and Selected Poems.* BOA Editions, 2006.
WHA-CP   *W. H. Auden, Collected Poems,* ed. E. Mendelson. Modern Library, 2007.
WillS   *The Oxford Shakespeare.* Oxford University Press, 2005.
WS-CP   *The Collected Poems of Wallace Stevens,* ed. John N. Serio and Chris Beyers. Vintage, 2015.

1. Sources of Delight: What We Respond to When We Respond to Poetry

Hopkins, Gerard Manley. "The Windhover." In *Poems and Prose of Gerard Manley Hopkins,* ed. W. H. Gardner. Penguin Classics, 1985.
Momaday, N. Scott. "Angle of Geese." In N. Scott Momaday, *Angle of Geese and Other Poems.* Godine, 1974.
Stevens, Wallace. "The Idea of Order at Key West." WS-CP.
Walcott, Derek. *Omeros.* Farrar Straus, 1990.
Weigl, Bruce. "Snowy Egret." In Bruce Weigl, *Song of Napalm.* Atlantic Monthly Press, 1988.

2. Some Poetic Strategies

Arnold, Matthew. "Dover Beach." In *Poems by Matthew Arnold.* Leopold Classical Library, 2016.
Ashbery, John. "Like a Sentence." In John Ashbery, *And the Stars Were Shining.* Farrar Straus, 1994.
Bishop, Elizabeth. "The Shampoo." EB-CP.
Bowers, Edgar. "The Mirror." In Edgar Bowers, *The Astronomers.* Swallow, 1965.
Eliot, T. S. "East Coker." TSE-CP.
Gunn, Thom. "The Bed." TG-CP.
H.D. "Oread" and "Sea Iris." HD-CP.
Lowell, Robert. "Water." RL-CP.
Paterson, Don. "The Error." In Don Paterson, *Rain.* Farrar Straus, 2009.
Stern, Gerald. "Glut." In Gerald Stern, *Save the Last Dance.* Norton, 2008.
Stevens, Wallace. "Earthy Anecdote." WS-CP.
Wilbur, Richard. "Blackberries for Amelia" and "Mind." RW-CP.

3. The Elusive Self: Poems and Personas

Auden, W. H. "As I Walked Out One Evening." WHA-CP.
Berryman, John. "Dream Song 93." In John Berryman, *The Dream Songs.* Farrar Straus, 2014.
Bogan, Louise. "Exhortation" and "Roman Fountain." LB-BE.

Brooks, Gwendolyn. "God Works in a Mysterious Way." EGB.

Cunningham, J. V. "Epigram." JVC-CP.

Dale, Peter. "The Terms." In Peter Dale, *Mortal Fire*. Ohio University Press, 1976.

Fields, Kenneth. "The Game Theorist." In Kenneth Fields, *The Other Walker*. Talisman Literary Research, 1971.

Frost, Robert. "Build Soil," "Desert Places," and "The Most of It." RF-CP.

Gunn, Thom. "Outside the Diner." TG-CP.

Housman, A. E. "To an Athlete Dying Young." In A. E. Housman, *Collected Poems*. Dead Authors Society, 2020.

Justice, Donald. "A Letter." In Donald Justice, *Collected Poems*. Knopf, 2004.

Kizer, Carolyn. "Bitch." In Carolyn Kizer, *Cool, Calm, & Collected: Poems, 1960–2000*. Copper Canyon, 2001.

Larkin, Philip. "Cut Grass." PL-CP.

Olds, Sharon. "The Knowing." In Sharon Olds, *Strike Sparks*. Knopf, 2004.

Plath, Sylvia. "Lady Lazareth." SP-CP.

Robinson, Edwin Arlington. "Eros Turannos." In Edwin Arlington Robinson, *Collected Poems*. Macmillan, 1937.

Sexton, Anne. "Angel of Clean Sheets." In Anne Sexton, *Complete Poems*. Houghton Mifflin, 1999.

Stevens, Wallace. "The Idea of Order at Key West" and "The Man Whose Pharynx Was Bad." WS-CP.

Teasdale, Sara. "Like Barley Bending." In Sara Teasdale, *Collected Poems*. Pantianos Classics, 2017.

Wilbur, Richard. "For the Student Strikers." RW-CP.

Yeats, W. B. "The Secrets of the Old." WBY-CP.

4. But Enough about Me: Poems without Personas

Auden, W. H. "Look, Stranger" and "The More Loving One." WHA-CP.

Bogan, Louise. "Roman Fountain" and "To an Artist, to Take Heart." LB-BE.

Burns, Robert. "To a Louse." In *Complete Poems and Songs of Robert Burns*. Geddes & Grosset, 2015.

Dickinson, Emily. "Further in Summer Than the Birds." ED-CP.

Eliot, T. S. "Burnt Norton." TSE-CP.

Glück, Louise. "The Winged Horse." LG-P.

Greville, Fulke. "Chorus Sacerdotum." FG-SP.

Gunn, Thom. "Berlin in Ruins." TG-CP.

Hecht, Anthony. "The Darkness and the Light Are Both Alike to Thee." In Anthony Hecht, *Collected Poems*, ed. Philip Hoy. Farrar Straus, 2003.

Hughes, Ted. "How to Paint a Water Lily." In Ted Hughes, *Collected Poems*. Farrar Straus, 2003.

Larkin, Philip. "Pigeons." PL-CP.

Paterson, Don. "The Poetry." In Don Paterson, *Rain*. Farrar Straus, 2009.

Ryan, Kay. "A Plain Ordinary Steel Needle Can Float on Pure Water." KR-NSP.

Stallings, A. E. "Actaeon." In A. E. Stallings, *Hapax*. Northwestern University Press, 2006.

Walcott, Derek. "Night Fishing." In *The Poetry of Derek Walcott, 1948–2013*. Farrar Straus, 2014.

5. All in the Family: Parents and Children in Today's Poetry

Bai Juyi, trans. Arthur Waley. "Remembering Golden Bells." In Arthur Waley, *Translations from the Chinese*. Knopf, 1941.

Bogan, Louise. "M., Singing." LB-BE.

Brooks, Gwendolyn. "The Mother." EGB.

Gioia, Dana. "Majority." In Dana Gioia, *Interrogations at Noon*. Graywolf, 2001.

Heaney, Seamus. "Follower." In Seamus Heaney, *Selected Poems 1966–1987*. Farrar Straus, 2014.

Jamie, Kathleen. "Moon." In Kathleen Jamie, *The Overhaul*. Picador, 2012.

Jarman, Mark. "Dressing My Daughters." In Mark Jarman, *Bone Fires: New and Selected Poems*. Sarabande, 2011.

Juster, A. M. "Fugitive Son." In A. M. Juster, *Wonder and Wrath*. Paul Dry, 2020.

Lowell, Robert. "Harriet." RL-CP.

Mason, David. "Swimmers on the Shore." In David Mason, *The Sound: New and Selected Poems*. Red Hen, 2018.

Millay, Edna St. Vincent. "Sonnet XII." In Edna St. Vincent Millay, *Collected Poems*. Harper, 2011. Paterson, Don. "The Swing." In Don Paterson, *Rain*. Farrar Straus, 2009.

Plath, Sylvia. "Morning Song." SP-CP.

Snodgrass, W. D. "Heart's Needle." WDS-NSP.

Stallings, A. E. "Whethering." In A. E. Stallings, *Like*. Farrar Straus, 2018.

Voigt, Ellen Bryant. "The Photograph." In Ellen Bryant Voigt, *Collected Poems*. Norton, 2023.

Winters, Yvor. "A Leave-Taking." In *Selected Poems of Yvor Winters*, ed. R. L. Barth. Swallow/Ohio University Press, 1999.

Wordsworth, William. "Intimations of Immortality." In *Collected Poems of William Wordsworth*. Ragged Hand, 2018.

Wyatt, Thomas. "They Flee from Me." In *Sir Thomas Wyatt: The Complete Poems*, ed. R. A. Rebholz. Penguin, 1978.

Yezzi, David. "Let." In David Yezzi, *More Things in Heaven: New and Selected Poems*. Measure, 2022.

6. Short of Breath: Poems in a Narrow Compass

Ammons, A. R. *Tape for the Turn of the Year.* In A. R. Ammons, *Tape for the Turn of the Year.* Norton, 1965.

Bishop, Elizabeth. "The Moose." EB-CP.

Brooks, Gwendolyn. "The Pool Players." EGB.

Campion, Thomas. "Follow, Follow." In *Campion's Works,* ed. Percival Vivian. Clarendon Press, 1966.

Creeley, Robert. "I Know a Man." In *Selected Poems of Robert Creeley.* University of California Press, 1991.

Cunningham, J. V. "To the Reader." JVC-CP.

Eliot, T. S. "The Waste Land." TSE-CP.

H.D. "Sea Iris." HD-CP.

Herrick, Robert. "Upon a Delaying Lady." In *The Poems of Robert Herrick.* Oxford University Press, 1965.

Menashe, Samuel. "Anonymous," "Eyes," "Pity Us," and "These Stone Steps." In *Samuel Menashe, New and Selected Poems,* ed. Christopher Ricks. Library of America, 2005.

Ryan, Kay. "The Best of It." KR-NSP.

Turnbull, Belle. "Brother Juniper" and "High Trail." In *Belle Turnbull,* ed. David Rothman and Jeffrey Villines. Pleiades, 2017.

Young, Kevin. "Hurricane Song." In *Kevin Young, Jelly Roll: A Blues.* Knopf, 2005.

7. The Phoenix Line: History of a Style

Auden, W. H. "Lullaby." WHA-CP.

Blake, William. "The Tyger." In William Blake, *Complete Poems.* Penguin, 1978.

Brooks, Gwendolyn. *The Anniad.* EGB.

Frost, Robert. "To the Thawing Wind." RF-CP.

Greville, Fulke. "All My Senses." FG-SP.

Jonson, Ben. "Hymn to Diana." In *Ben Jonson,* ed. Ian Donaldson. Oxford University Press, 1985.

———. *The Staple of News,* ed. Anthony Parr. Manchester University Press, 2002.

Keats, John. "Fancy." In John Keats, *Complete Poems.* Penguin, 1977.

Larkin, Philip. "First Sight." PL-CP.

Shakespeare, William. Ariel's song from *The Tempest* and "The Phoenix and the Turtle." WillS.

Yeats, W. B. "Under Ben Bulben." WBY-CP.

8. On the Translation of Poetry

Baudelaire, Charles. "Le Squelette Laboureur." CB-FE.

Borges, Jorge Luis. "HO." In Jorge Luis Borges, *Poesía complete.* Debolsillo, 2018.

Dante. *The Inferno of Dante*, trans. Robert Pinsky. Farrar Straus, 1994.

———. *La Divina Commedia*. Mondadori, 2022.

Goethe, J. W. von. *Faust*. Anaconda Verlag, 2012.

———. *Faust, Part I*, trans. Zsuzsanna Ozsváth & Frederick Turner. Deep Vellum, 2021.

Levine, Philip. "They Feed They Lion." In Philip Levine, *They Feed They Lion*. Macmillan, 1972.

Mezey, Robert. "NW." In Robert Mezey, *Collected Poems, 1952–1999*. University of Arkansas Press, 2000.

Rilke, Rainer Maria. "Archaic Torso of Apollo." Author's translation.

———. Excerpt from *Das Buch von der Armut und vom Tode*. In Rainer Maria Rilke, *Das Stundenbuch*. Hofenberg, 2016.

Valéry, Paul. "Le Cimetière marin" and "Les Pas." PPV.

Winters, Yvor. "Skeletons Digging." CB-FE.

9. Serpent in the Tree: Poetry of a Fallen World

Auden, W. H. "Danse Macabre." WHA-CP.

Cunningham, J. V. "Haecceity." JVC-CP.

Milton, John. *Paradise Lost* iii,11. 203–212, 103–106. Penguin, 2016.

Valéry, Paul. "Ébauche d'un serpent." PPV.

10. The Curator as Oracle: A Guide to *The Harlem Gallery*

Tolson, Melvin. *The Harlem Gallery*. In *"Harlem Gallery" and Other Poems of Melvin B. Tolson*, ed. Raymond Nelson. University of Virginia Press, 1999.

11. Enter at Your Own Risk: Poems of Vijay Seshadri

Seshadri, Vijay. *That Was Now, This Is Then*. Graywolf, 2020.

12. Formalists against the Tide: What They Learned from the Tide

Bishop, Elizabeth. "Paris, 7 A.M." EB-CP.

Bogan, Louise. "Old Countryside." LB-BE.

Dickinson, Emily. "The difference between Despair." ED-CP.

Eliot, T. S. "The Love Song of J. Alfred Prufrock" and "The Waste Land." TSE-CP.

Frost, Robert Frost. "A Girl's Garden" and "My Butterfly." RF-CP.

Lowell, Robert. "Hawthorne" and "Returning." RL-CP.

Nemerov, Howard. "For Robert Frost, in the Autumn, in Vermont" and "The Mud Turtle." In *Collected Poems of Howard Nemerov*. University of Chicago Press, 1981.

O'Hara, Frank. "The Day Lady Died." In *Collected Poems of Frank O'Hara*. University of California Press, 1995.

Pound, Ezra. "The Tree." In *Ezra Pound: Poems & Translations*. Library of America, 2003.

Roethke, Theodore. "The Far Field." In *Collected Poems of Theodore Roethke*. Anchor, 1975.

Snodgrass, W. D. "A Separation Anthem." WDS-NSP.

Stevens, Wallace. "Disillusionment of Ten O'Clock," "Mozart, 1935," and "Sunday Morning." WS-CP.

Williams, William Carlos. "By the Road to the Contagious Hospital." WCW-CP.

13. Putting on the Style

Eliot, T. S. "The Waste Land." TSE-CP.

Frost, Robert. "Acquainted with the Night." RF-CP.

Glück, Louise, "The Empty Glass." LG-P.

Shakespeare, William. *King Lear*. WillS.

Steele, Timothy. "Joanna, Wading." In Timothy Steele, *Toward the Winter Solstice: New Poems*. Swallow/Ohio University Press, 2006.

Warren, Deborah. "Eleven." In Deborah Warren, *Zero Meridian*. Ivan R. Dee, 2004.

Warren, Rosanna. "Interior at Petworth." In Rosanna Warren, *Each Leaf Shines Separate*. Norton, 1984.

Williams, William Carlos. "The Yachts." WCW-CP.

Wizansky, Margot. "Shopping for Black Slacks," *Think Journal*, 13.1 (2023), 18.

14. Where Do We Come From? What Are We? Where Are We Going?

Eliot, T. S. "The Love Song of J. Alfred Prufrock" and "The Waste Land." TSE-CP.

Foy, John. "At Sea (*after paintings by Piet Mondrian*)." https://www.literarymatters.org/14-2-at-sea/.

Ginsberg, Allen. "Howl." In Allen Ginsberg, *Collected Poems, 1947–1997*. Harper, 2006.

Kweli, Talib. "Respiration" (co-written with Yasiin Bey). https://www.azlyrics.com/lyrics/blackstar/respiration.html.

Machado, Aditi. "now." In Aditi Machado, *Now*. Sputnik & Fizzle Chapbook Series 2, 2022.

Pardlo, Gregory. "Double Dutch." In Gregory Pardlo, *Totem*. American Poetry Review, 2007.

Pound, Ezra. "Canto LXXXI." In *The Cantos of Ezra Pound*. New Directions, 1996.

Wadud, Asiya. "Mandible Wishbone Solvent." In Asiya Wadud, *Mandible Wishbone Solvent*. University of Chicago Press, 2024.

Index of Names

Ammons, A. R., 92–93
Aquinas, Thomas, 130, 138
Armstrong, Louis, 151
Arnold, Matthew, 23
Ashbery, John, 30–32, 195
Auden, W. H., 37, 61, 62, 110, 138–41, 169
Austen, Jane, 63, 123

Bai Juyi, 70
Banville, John, 81
Baudelaire, Charles, 112, 114, 121, 122
Berg, Stephen, 178
Berryman, John, 42–43, 49, 50–51, 178
Bey, Yasiin (Mos Def), 213n
Bishop, Elizabeth, 25, 51, 67, 89, 96, 181, 183
Blake, William, 32n, 103–4, 110, 137, 203
Bly, Robert, 32n
Bogan, Louise, 35, 37, 39, 47n, 50, 60, 65, 126n, 180
Borges, Jorge Luis, 119–21
Bowers, Edgar, 28
Bradstreet, Anne, 63
Brahms, Johannes, 125n
Brautigan, Richard, 49
Bridges, Robert, 142n
Brooks, Gwendolyn, 38, 72, 94, 109, 110, 183
Browning, Elizabeth Barrett, 34, 63
Browning, Robert, 65, 172

Burns, Robert, 49
Burt, Stephanie (née Stephen), 204
Byron, George Gordon, 158

Campion, Thomas, 82–83
Cassirer, Ernst, 20
Chagall, Marc, 150
Chattaway, Thurland, 198n
Ciardi, John, 116
Cicero, 203
Cobb, Jelani, 213n
Coleridge, Samuel Taylor, 63
Corneille, Pierre, 114
Crane, Hart, 49, 194
Creeley, Robert, 93–94
Cunningham, J. V., vii, 41, 87, 90, 130

da Vinci, Leonardo, 208
Dale, Peter, 40
Dante Alighieri, 115, 116–17
Daryush, Elizabeth, 178
Davie, Donald, 17, 18, 30
Day, John, 194
Def, Mos. *See* Bey, Yasiin
Dickey, James, 174
Dickinson, Emily, 48n, 53–54, 55, 178
Dove, Rita, 157n
Dryden, John, 158